The Secrets of Ancient Tombs

Tutankhamun's Tomb and Other Ancient Tombs

Federico Puigdevall

Cavendish
Square

New York

This edition published in 2018 by Cavendish Square Publishing, LLC
243 5th Avenue, Suite 136, New York, NY 10016

First Edition

Website: cavendishsq.com

This publication represents the opinions and views of the author based on his or her personal experience, knowledge, and research. The information
in this book serves as a general guide only. The author and publisher have used their best efforts in preparing this book and disclaim liability rising
directly or indirectly from the use and application of this book.

All websites were available and accurate when this book was sent to press.

Cataloging-in-Publication Data

Names: Puigdevall, Federico, 1955-.
Title: The secrets of ancient tombs / Federico Puigdevall.
Description: New York : Cavendish Square, 2018. | Series: The secrets of history | Includes bibliographical references and index.
Identifiers: ISBN 9781502632647 (library bound) | ISBN 9781502632630 (ebook)
Subjects: LCSH: Tombs--Juvenile literature. | Excavations (Archaeology)--Juvenile literature. | Civilization, Ancient--Juvenile literature.
Classification: LCC CC77.B8 P85 2018 | DDC 930.1--dc23

Editorial Director: David McNamara
Editor: Erica Grove
Associate Art Director: Amy Greenan
Production Coordinator: Karol Szymczuk

Original Idea Sol90 Publishing
Project Management Nuria Cicero
Editorial Coordination Diana Malizia
Editorial Team Alberto Hernández, Virginia Iris Fernández, Mar Valls, Marta de la Serna, Sebastián Romeu. Maximiliano Ludueña, Carlos Bodyadjan,
Doris Elsa Bustamante, Tania Domenicucci, Andrea Giacobone, Constanza Guariglia, Joaquín Hidalgo, Hernán López Winne.
Proofreaders Marta Kordon, Edgardo D'Elio
Design Fabián Cassan
Layout Laura Ocampo, Carolina Berdiñas, Clara Miralles, Paola Fornasaro, Mariana Marx, Pablo Alarcón

Printed in the United States of America

The Findings of the 20th Century

The Mysterious Boy Who Became Pharaoh

P.H.D. C. Ad.
132

GRATIS.— تعطى مجانا— إدارة ١٢٢

CERTIFICAT DE DÉCÈS.— شـــهادة وفاة

Le soussigné, après l'avoir examiné, certifie que :

LO nommé *The Rt: Hon: Henry, George, Kornhofu, Earl of Carno.*

What Is the Curse of Tutankhamun?

What Caused His Death?

The Findings of the 20th Century

On November 4, 1922 an Englishman, Howard Carter, made a discovery in Egypt's Valley of the Kings which would change the face of archaeology for good. Here, for the first time in history, a scientific excavator found himself confronted by the sealed doorway of an intact royal tomb. It proved to be the burial of a boy-king, Tutankhamen, crammed from floor to ceiling with "gold—everywhere the glint of gold." It was a treasure of such extraordinary bullion worth that it shook the world.

Carter's long years of search had at last paid off, but the situation soon began to sour. The excavator and his patron, Lord Carnarvon, quarrelled bitterly; not long after the fifth Earl was dead, supposed victim of "pharaoh's curse." Carter, ill-suited to juggle the conflicting demands of archaeology and diplomacy, was left to cope alone. Against a background of jealousy, greed and political unrest matters spiralled rapidly downwards, out of control. The architect of Egypt's triumph was sacked and humiliated; he would return to complete the clearance only because it was a job no-one else wanted.

By his discovery Carter seemed to have loosed a genie from its bottle. Almost at once, assessing the tomb and seeing what was at stake, the Egyptian Government took steps to impose far stricter control over its country's rich cultural heritage. The old 50:50 division of finds came to an end, closing many excavations down. Archaeology in Egypt was shaken to its foundations.

Popular expectations of the subject, too, became hopelessly skewed, with Tutankhamen's treasure now the unrealistic standard by which archaeological success—or failure—would in future be gauged. Reaction set in as Carter's colleagues, their currency potsherds rather than gold, felt the threat. Separated by a chasm from the everyday realities of digging in Egypt, Carter's amazing discovery would find itself quietly undermined as vulgar and superficial, and not at all the stuff of serious scholarly research—a peculiar prejudice which Egyptology has taken years to shake off.

Today, rightfully, Tutankhamen occupies academic center-stage, with the theories coming thick and fast. Scientifically, in the wake of CT-scanning and DNA analysis there are new thoughts about the young king's place in Amarna's complex family tree, how in reality he looked, and how he might have died. Historically, we now recognize the part Tutankhamen and his agents played in the dismantling of Akhenaten's capital, and the transfer to and final reinterment of the Amarna dead in the Valley of the Kings. Archaeologically, we are beginning to comprehend better than ever before the activities of those who plundered the tomb—both in antiquity and in the more recent past.

But much more than that: we discern at last the essential nature of pharaoh's burial—from minor details of iconography and text. These reveal the startling reality that most of the boy-king's treasure had never been intended for him at all. Shrines, sarcophagus, coffins, mask and mummy trappings—virtually all were secondhand, originally prepared for his beautiful stepmother, Nefertiti, in her newly discerned role as Akhenaten's co-regent. Nefertiti: the queen-pharaoh whose own tomb still waits to be found, perhaps within meters of Tutankhamen himself...

After the fanfare surrounding its brilliant discovery and the ensuing decades of neglect, the boy-king's tomb is at last acknowledged not only as one of civilization's greatest artistic treasures, but as one of the most significant, untapped repositories of raw evidence to have come down to us from the ancient world—a crucial catalyst for understanding and progress. If advances to date have been impressive, without doubt the tomb's yield for the future will be very much greater still.

Nicholas Reeves

Archaeologist and historian specializing in the Valley of the Kings and the tomb of Tutankhamen. He graduated in Ancient History from University College London in 1979, and received his PhD in Egyptology from Durham University in 1984.

HIDDEN CHAMBER
In the foreground is the modest
entrance to the tomb of Tutankhamun,
which is in front of the mound that
provides access to the tomb of
Ramses VI.

The Mysterious Boy Who Became Pharaoh

Tutankhamen lived 23 centuries ago, and died at only 19 years of age. The "resurrection" of the Egyptian Pharaoh took place in 1922 at the hand of English Egyptologist Howard Carter. Tutankhamen's tomb became one of the greatest archaeological finds in history.

T he arrival of Italian Giovanni Battista Belzoni (1778–1823) to the Egyptian port of Alexandria in June of 1815 paved the way for the plunder of the ancient sites, in the service of the British Consul. Belzoni, an adventurer nearly two meters (6 ft 6 in) tall, went from being a giant strongman in fairs and circuses to raiding temples and tombs. Perhaps his circus number, the human pyramid, which involved lifting twelve men as if they were nothing, gave him the idea of going to Egypt and lifting the treasures of the Pharaohs. His Herculean exploits notably include bringing the bust of Ramses II, weighing seven tons, and the obelisk of Ptolemy IX, seven meters

(almost 23 ft) tall, to London. His work also included gaining entrance to the interior of the Pyramid of Khafre and the excavation of the Temple of Abu Simbel, which was covered with sand. In the Valley of the Kings, he penetrated a labyrinth of tombs, most without mummies, but full of mysterious symbols and drawings, such as that of Seti I.

CHAMPOLLION, A VISIONARY

After Belzoni left, returning to Europe in 1819 convinced that there was nothing left to discover in the Valley of the Kings, the Englishman John Gardner Wilkinson was the first to read the names of the pharaohs using the Champollion method and to number the known tombs (in 1827). Jean-François Champollion's visit to Egypt a year later, from August of 1828 to

December of 1829, made it possible to unravel the true significance of the Valley. "I am a man who has just been resurrected," he stated, in the spirit of going beyond established knowledge. He was able to establish that the Valley of the Kings was the necropolis of the pharaohs of Thebes. And he was ahead of his time, stating that the tombs of the eighteenth dynasty would be found there. After Champollion's death, only a few occasional adventurers filled his role as illustrators of the marvels of ancient Egypt. The Valley of the Kings appeared to have been forgotten. Not even the French Egyptologist Auguste Mariette (1821–1881) paid attention to the region, although he did try to end the trafficking of antiquities and created the first Egyptian museum in Cairo. Another

THE TREASURE
The funerary mask of Tutankhamen is the most outstanding piece that was found in his tomb.

Frenchman, Gaston Maspero (1846–1916) made history as the director of the Egyptian Antiquities Service, founded in 1881, and brought new life into the Valley of the Kings. He made his way into a tomb with forty mummies, nine of which were Pharaohs of Thebes, brought there during the time of the Pharaohs to avoid plundering.

THE AMARNA LETTERS
Meanwhile, in Amarna, 248.55 miles (400 km) from the Valley of the Kings, other sensational discoveries were made. Once named Akhenaten, what is today called Amarna was once the capital of the Egyptian empire, and was founded by Akhenaten—considered to be the father of Tutankhamen—in order to consecrate the worship of Aten (the sun). There, in 1887, some rural Egyptians were looking for mud to make adobe bricks when they found, instead, hundreds of clay tablets with missives between Pharaohs and kings of other regions. For a while,

these archaeological treasures were plundered slowly and distributed on the antiquities black market, but then science took an interest in the matter. The first archaeologist to attempt recovery of the pieces was the legendary William M. Flinders Petrie, in 1891. These tablets, which today number some 400 (half are housed in a museum in Berlin), provide very valuable information about the time in which Tutankhamen lived, as well as his ancestors and predecessors on the throne,

the Pharaohs Akhenaten and Amenhotep III. They are written in cuneiform Akkadian, the lingua franca of the time, and total about 300 letters. Known as "the Amarna letters," their finding raises a range of questions. Many of the messages are addressed to "the pharaoh," without additional information, which makes it difficult to place them chronologically. In addition, the use of Akkadian by the Egyptian scribes makes it difficult to understand the texts, since the use of that

WIFE AND SISTER
Ankhesenamun, the wife of Tutankhamen, rubs oil on the Pharaoh in this relief that was found on the back of the king's golden throne, in his tomb. Daughter of Akhenaten and Nefertiti, she was Tutankhamen's half-sister.

THE FIND
Howard Carter (kneeling) observes the sarcophagus of the Pharaoh, which had been covered by four shrines, for the first time, in early 1924. Lord Carnarvon had died eight months earlier and never got to see the mummy.

language was not very customary, and more than a few errors were made.

RESURGENCE OF THE VALLEY
The Valley of the Kings would be reborn from its ashes as the 20th century approached. The Englishman Howard Carter, only 17 years old, arrived in Egypt in 1891. His father and grandfather were illustrators, and he soon figured out how to earn a place in the world of archaeology, drawing the tombs and familiarizing himself with the environment of

the pharaohs. It was a time of extraordinary finds including Amenhotep II, Amenhotep III, and other kings, and led to an invasion of tourists. From the city of Luxor, ancient Thebes, there were continuous excursions to the burial grounds of the valley, on the other bank of the Nile, some 3.1 miles (5 km) to the west. In 1900, Gaston Maspero appointed the young Carter, a fully self-taught and now well-known archaeologist, as Chief Inspector of the Egyptian Antiquities Service (EAS).

In 1902, a wealthy American named Theodore M. Davis (1837–1915), a retired attorney and art collector, decided to launch a pharaonic adventure in Egypt. Gaston Maspero was greatly relieved to have money coming into the battered arches of the Antiquities Service, in exchange for granting an excavation permit through 1915.

ARCHAEOLOGY FEVER
That valley from another age "that loves the silence," protected by a mountain

Continued on page 16 ▶

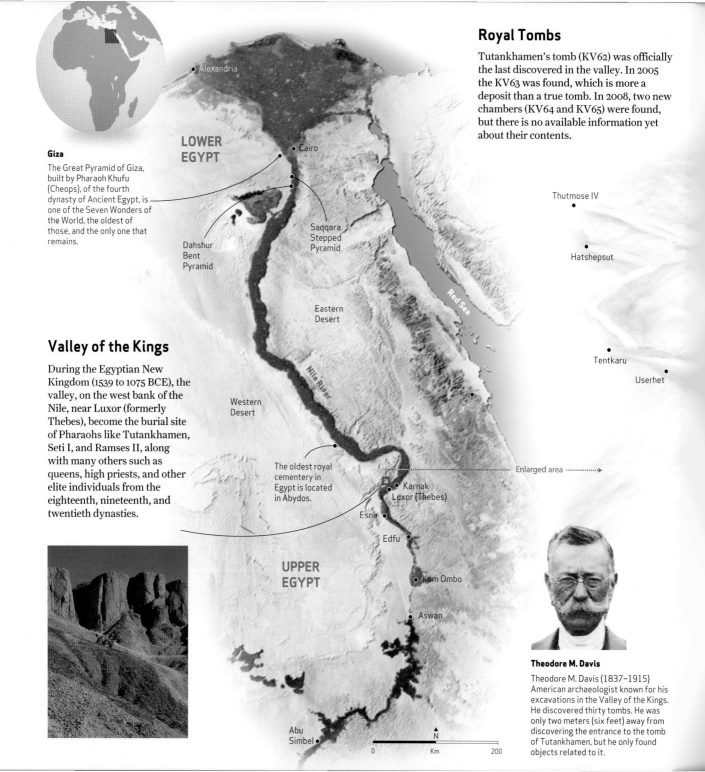

Royal Tombs

Tutankhamen's tomb (KV62) was officially the last discovered in the valley. In 2005 the KV63 was found, which is more a deposit than a true tomb. In 2008, two new chambers (KV64 and KV65) were found, but there is no available information yet about their contents.

Giza

The Great Pyramid of Giza, built by Pharaoh Khufu (Cheops), of the fourth dynasty of Ancient Egypt, is one of the Seven Wonders of the World, the oldest of those, and the only one that remains.

Alexandria

LOWER EGYPT

Cairo

Saqqara Stepped Pyramid

Dahshur Bent Pyramid

Thutmose IV

Hatshepsut

Eastern Desert

Red Sea

Tentkaru

Userhet

Valley of the Kings

During the Egyptian New Kingdom (1539 to 1075 BCE), the valley, on the west bank of the Nile, near Luxor (formerly Thebes), become the burial site of Pharaohs like Tutankhamen, Seti I, and Ramses II, along with many others such as queens, high priests, and other elite individuals from the eighteenth, nineteenth, and twentieth dynasties.

Western Desert

Nile River

The oldest royal cementery in Egypt is located in Abydos.

Enlarged area

Karnak
Luxor (Thebes)

Esna

Edfu

Kom Ombo

UPPER EGYPT

Aswan

Theodore M. Davis

Theodore M. Davis (1837–1915) American archaeologist known for his excavations in the Valley of the Kings. He discovered thirty tombs. He was only two meters (six feet) away from discovering the entrance to the tomb of Tutankhamen, but he only found objects related to it.

Abu Simbel

N

0   Km   200

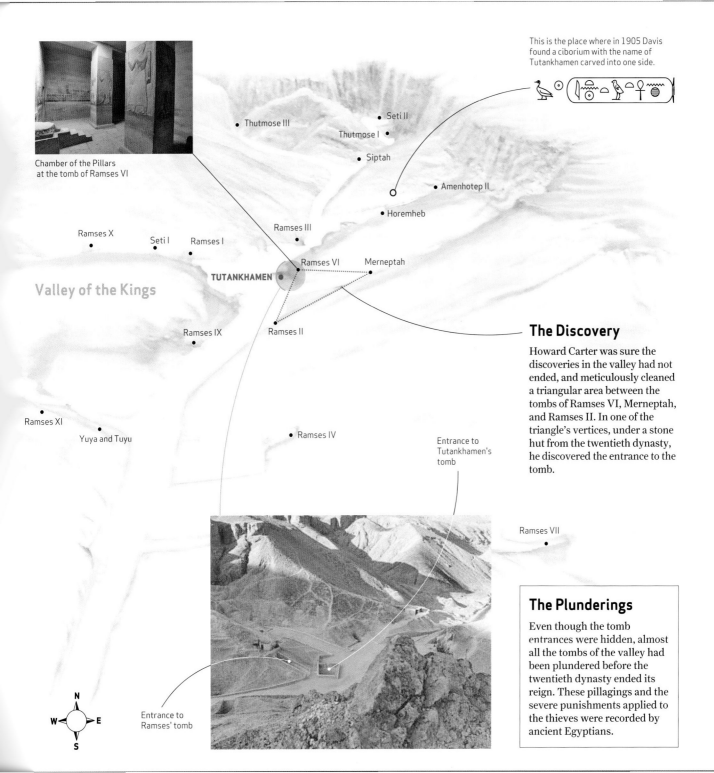

Chamber of the Pillars
at the tomb of Ramses VI

This is the place where in 1905 Davis found a ciborium with the name of Tutankhamen carved into one side.

Thutmose III

Seti II

Thutmose I

Siptah

Amenhotep II

Horemheb

Ramses X

Ramses III

Seti I

Ramses I

Ramses VI

Merneptah

Valley of the Kings

TUTANKHAMEN

Ramses IX

Ramses II

The Discovery

Howard Carter was sure the discoveries in the valley had not ended, and meticulously cleaned a triangular area between the tombs of Ramses VI, Merneptah, and Ramses II. In one of the triangle's vertices, under a stone hut from the twentieth dynasty, he discovered the entrance to the tomb.

Ramses XI

Yuya and Tuyu

Ramses IV

Entrance to Tutankhamen's tomb

Ramses VII

The Plunderings

Even though the tomb entrances were hidden, almost all the tombs of the valley had been plundered before the twentieth dynasty ended its reign. These pillagings and the severe punishments applied to the thieves were recorded by ancient Egyptians.

N
W · E
S

Entrance to Ramses' tomb

peak in the form of a pyramid, saw the arrival of a team of tomb hunters who stirred up every corner of the land. Howard Carter, as Chief Inspector of the area, occupied himself with archaeological management. His outstanding work in the necropolis of Thebes led Maspero, in 1904, to set him up as Inspectorate of Lower Egypt, the jewel where Memphis and Giza shone. It was bittersweet, as he had to bid farewell to the beloved valley. The following year, he confronted a group of drunk French tourists who were very influential in diplomatic circles. As the affair unraveled, Carter was obligated to leave his post. His only alternative was to return to illustration and painting, combined with working as a guide and antiquities dealer, so as to get by in Cairo. But the Valley of the Kings stayed in his thoughts. Maspero, feeling guilty about having terminated his valuable services, contacted the English aristocrat George Herbert (1866–1923), the Fifth Earl of Carnarvon, who was looking for an excavation manager. Thus began, in 1907, the story of a pair that would come to find glory.

Initially, they obtained permission to work in a less promising area of Thebes. But Carter never took his eye off of the necropolis of Thebes. The unknown Pharaoh Tutankhamen had been in the sights of the English Egyptologist since the discovery of an alabaster cup with his name, made by the Davis team in 1905.

While Carter and his team reaped several small successes (tombs of nobles, temple ruins, and objects of notable interest), the days of Davis' archaeological ambitions seemed to be numbered. After twelve consecutive winters, with the discovery of more than thirty tombs and the possible mummy of the disputed reformer Akhenaten to his credit, the old American reached the conclusion that both he and the valley were exhausted.

CARTER'S HOUR

Carter obtained permission to excavate in the Valley of the Kings in 1914. The First World War halted the start of his new adventure. At the end of 1917, he went to work. First, he had to clear away the enormous mountain of rubble that had accumulated in the area and carry it out of the valley. Carter dreamed of Tutankhamen day and night. After five years of fruitless searching, the patience and money of Lord Carnarvon were also exhausted. The perseverance of Carter the Egyptologist, who was willing to bear all of the expenses and risk losing everything he had in the attempt, convinced Carnarvon the aristocrat to give him one more chance.

The last drive began on November 1, 1922. Carter had full confidence in the American Egyptologist Herbert Winlock, who believed he saw embalming residue from the funeral of Tutankhamen in the contents of a small tomb discovered by Davis in 1907. With the spirit of a visionary, Carter began the seemingly hopeless operation of searching just below the entrance to the tomb of Ramses VI. After three days of excavation, the first step of a stairway covered with rubble appeared. Once it was clean, Carter went down 16 stairs and arrived at a sealed door. Through a small hole he made, he could see a passage filled with stones. Keeping his composure, he ordered the entrance to the tomb closed and sent a telegram to Lord Carnarvon to report the finding. On November 26, Carter and Lord Carnarvon stood in front of the second sealed door at the end of the passage.

The name of Tutankhamen left no doubt. Another hole allowed Carter to poke his head through and illuminate the area with a lamp. Silence reigned. Lord Carnarvon broke it, asking Carter, "Can you see anything?" Carter, dazzled by the shining gold, responded, "Yes, wonderful things."

That antechamber opened into an

W. M. Flinders Petrie
1853–1942

A pioneer of archaeology, and one of the most important Egyptologists in history. A young Carter, 18 years old, trained at his side for one year during the excavations of Amarna. Flinders Petrie worked in Egypt for more than 45 years and wrote nearly one hundred books. Although he was self-taught, and is not among the pioneers of Egyptology, many consider him the father of modern excavation. He was very critical of the quality of work performed by his predecessors.

METHODS Flinders Petrie created excavation and object dating techniques that are still in use today.

Harry Burton
1879–1940

A British photographer, he worked for Theodore Davis in the Valley of the Kings. As Howard Carter's official photographer, he took more than 1,400 snapshots of Tutankhamen's tomb, which are among the best works of archaeological photography in history.

DOCUMENTATION Burton spent eight years photographing and even filming the treasures of Tutankhamen.

◀ From page 13

Continued on page 20 ▶

Howard Carter

Like one of his mentors, Flinders Petrie, and like Heinrich Schliemann—who discovered Troy—Carter did not undertake academic study. Also like them, his findings made him immortal, despite the disdain with which he was viewed by the scientific community. He began his career as an illustrator (like his father), an occupation that was very useful in his profession. His obstinate temperament, "that my enemies like to call bad character," gave rise to more than a few problems in his early times in Egypt. In 1909, Lord Carnarvon took him on as a specialist to undertake the excavations he sponsored. The rest is history. Carter appears to have thrown all of his passion into archaeological research: he never married, had no children, and is not known to have had amorous relationships. In his will, he left all of his possessions to a niece. It took him ten years to classify the objects from Tutankhamen's tomb, and his report, in six volumes, remained unfinished on the date of his death from lymphatic cancer.

DISCOVERER Carter's stubbornness would not allow him to abandon the search for the tomb of the "boy king," even after long years of unfruitful searching. Finally, he earned his long-awaited reward, surpassing imagination.

1874–1939

"It was our great privilege to find the most significant collection of Egyptian antiquities that have ever seen the light of day." H.C.

Zahi Hawass

Probably the most renowned Egyptologist of modern times. Starting in 2002, he acted as General Secretary to the Egyptian Supreme Council of Antiquities, a position he left at the end of 2009, when he was named Vice Minister of Culture. Among his most outstanding discoveries are the identification of the mummy of Hatshepsut and the finding of new passages in the Great Pyramid. He ordered the CT scan performed on the mummy of Tutankhamen in 2005.

DEDICATION Hawass has worked arduously to restore the treasures of Ancient Egypt—dispersed in different museums around the world—to their country of origin.

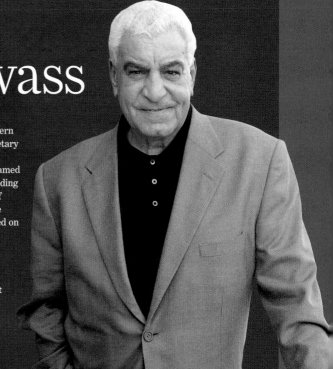

Tutankhamen's Tomb

This building is very small for being the final resting place of a pharaoh. It was not intended for it to be the young king's tomb. It resembles the structure of other tombs in the valley: A gallery ends in an anteroom that links with the burial chamber. Two side chambers have been identified as the "annex" and the "treasure chamber."

The Lost Tomb

It was a matter of luck that Tutankhamen's tomb remained intact. The burial chamber of the young king was built in the King's valley; 200 years later the Egyptians carved the tomb of Pharaoh Ramses VI directly above it. This construction covered Tutankhamen's mausoleum with stones.

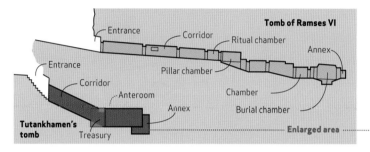

Tomb of Ramses VI
- Entrance
- Corridor
- Ritual chamber
- Annex
- Pillar chamber
- Chamber
- Burial chamber

Tutankhamen's tomb
- Entrance
- Corridor
- Anteroom
- Annex
- Treasury

Enlarged area →

ENTRANCE

On November 24 1922, archaeologist Howard Carter discovered, after five years of research, the entrance to Tutankhamen's tomb, hidden in the rocky soil of the Valley of the Kings.

ANTEROOM

The whole chamber was sealed in by walls. When the archaeologist Carter passed the first door, he found a room full of Pharaoh's objects, many of them made of carved gold or wood.

1,7 m

2 m

THE CORRIDOR

Both the corridor and the staircases were covered with stone rubble, probably a result of the excavation. There were also valuable items on the floor, apparently left there during an attempted robbery.

THE TREASURE

Crossing the burial chamber, and through an open door, is the treasury. A statue of Anubis guards the entrance and the Canopic Shrine, protected by four goddesses.

Canopic Chest

It contains the vital organs of the Pharaoh. The liver, lungs, stomach and intestines were removed from the body to avoid their decomposing inside the mummy.

Canopic chest

Egyptian goddess

Golden chest
It held four coffers or "jars"

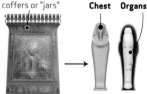

Chest   Organs

Why are the objects in the various chambers of the tomb so disorderly?

enigmas

Before even entering the tomb, Carter realized (because of a plaster patch on the wall) that it had been desecrated. His suspicions were confirmed when he found out that there were valuable objects missing and that it was significantly disturbed. It was obvious that thieves had tried to commit a robbery. It was more difficult to understand why the officers that came to clean up the tomb did so in such a negligent manner, as if they had been working in a hurry.

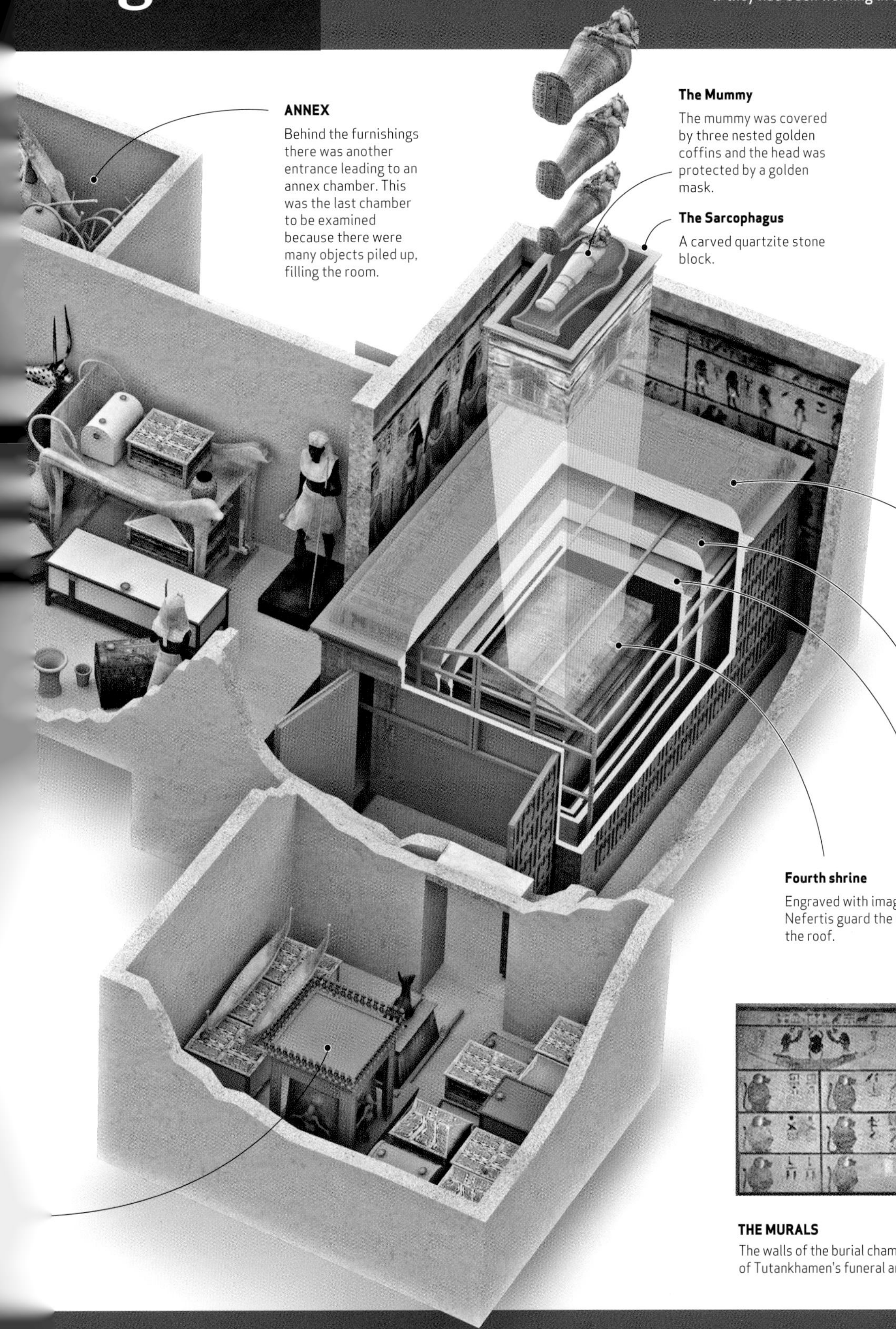

ANNEX

Behind the furnishings there was another entrance leading to an annex chamber. This was the last chamber to be examined because there were many objects piled up, filling the room.

The Mummy

The mummy was covered by three nested golden coffins and the head was protected by a golden mask.

The Sarcophagus

A carved quartzite stone block.

The Burial Chamber

The main chamber of the tomb, containing the Pharaoh's coffin, was hidden behind a sealed wall. The entrance had two life-size statues of Tutankhamen: one representing the young king and the other his Ka or soul.

Outer shrine

The outer shrine was made of carved cedar inlaid with blue faience. It was decorated with protective symbols.

Second shrine

A wooden shell covered with a layer of linen.

Third shrine

Covered in gold leaf, with religious inscriptions.

Fourth shrine

Engraved with images of the gods. Isis and Nefertis guard the doors and Nut and Horus the roof.

THE MURALS

The walls of the burial chamber are decorated with depictions of Tutankhamen's funeral and journey to the underworld.

Nefertiti: mother-in-law and stepmother

For decades, an alternative Hypotheses of the genealogy of Tutankhamen postulated that Nefertiti, the Great Royal Wife of Akhenaten, could have been the mother of the young Pharaoh. However, most Egyptologists believe Kiya (second wife of Akhenaten) gave birth to him. Nevertheless, both hypotheses appear to have lost strength in recent times, since it is known that the parents of Tutankhamen were siblings by both father and mother. Nefertiti, on the other hand, is the mother of Tutankhamen's wife, Ankhesenamun. But Nefertiti presents her own enigmas. Along with Cleopatra, she is one of the most famous women of Ancient Egypt, and a synonym for beauty (her name means "the beautiful one has arrived"). Her origins are unclear, and some think she may not have been of Egyptian origin. It is believed that she had a active role during the reign of Akhenaten. Some Egyptologists even believe she governed as Pharaoh. Much of her renown comes from the bust found in 1912 by German archaeologist Ludwig Borchardt in the workshop of the royal sculptor Thutmose. This sculpture did not escape controversy: the bust is found today in the Neues Museum of Berlin, and the Egyptian government claims that it was pilfered from the country by fraudulent means, and demands its return. The art historian Henri Stierlin published a book in 2009 (*Le buste de Néfertiti: Une imposture de l'égyptologie?*) where he proposes that the sculpture is a twentieth century fraud, with Art Nouveau characteristics. Recent examinations of the bust have shown test faces under the actual one, which is evidence of its legitimacy.

ICON OF BEAUTY
The immutable face of Nefertiti. The absence of the eye is another unknown: is its absence due to the artist's decision?

The king's mother, an unresolved mystery

DNA tests performed on various mummies in 2007, made public in February of 2010, determined with full certainty that the mother of Tutankhamen was the "young lady" from tomb KV35. The other mummy in the tomb, the "old lady," has been identified conclusively as Queen Tiye, wife of Amenhotep III and mother of Akhenaten (and therefore grandmother of Tutankhamen). In 2003, Egyptologist Joann Fletcher identified the "young lady" as Nefertiti, and posed the Hypotheses that the violent wound on her face was due to a postmortem blow meant to "desecrate" the body of the wife of the "heretic pharaoh," Akhenaten. The DNA tests, however, determined that the blow was received while she was alive, and, with all probability, was the cause of death. In addition to the mystery about the identity of this royal Egyptian character, the question arises: why was the "young lady" murdered, and who killed her?

THE MATERNAL FACE
The mummy of Tutankhamen's mother was identified in 2010. Her face is deformed from a mortal blow.

annex, an open room bursting with extraordinary objects. It was in a disorderly state, giving the impression of a frustrated or small scale robbery. Years of work were ahead to bring order out of all of that material, but at 2:00 pm on February 17, 1923, Carter entered the burial chamber. A grandiose shrine occupied almost the entire

◀ *From page 16*

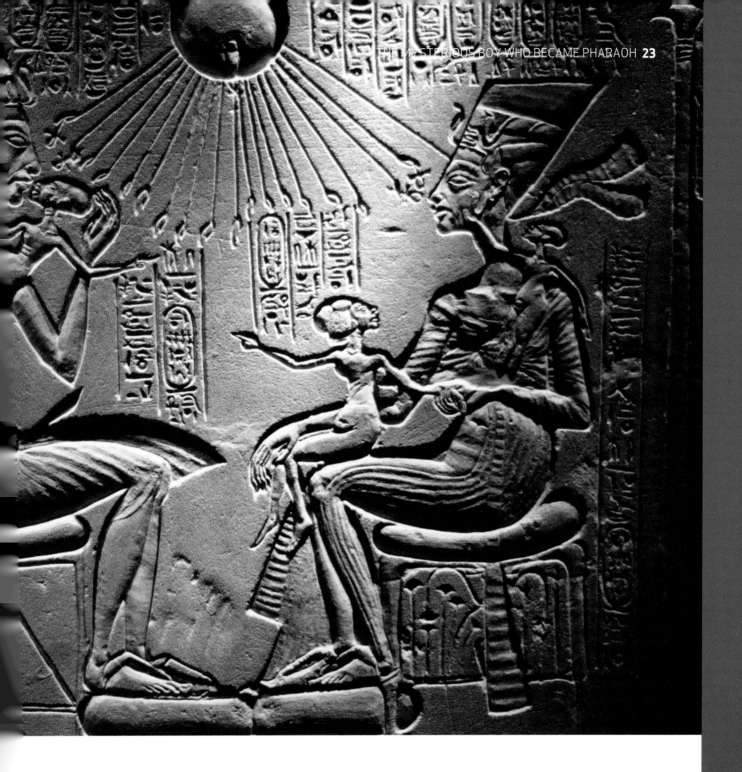

space of an intact location, with walls and ceiling painted in the manner of an open book. Just to the side was another magnificent surprise: the treasure chamber. On February 3, 1924, the sarcophagus of Tutankhamen, which held three nested coffins, was seen. Inside the coffins, gold masks covered the face and arms of the mummy, wrapped in linen cloths. Lord Carnarvon, who had died on April 5 of the previous year, never came to see the most famous object from his last Egyptian adventure. The specter of a supposed "curse of Tutankhamen" fed popular morbid curiosity. Carter had more luck. He died at 64 years old, perhaps disappointed at not having fulfilled his promise to find the tomb of Alexander the Great. He was buried without fanfare in a London cemetery. On his gravestone is written: "May your spirit live, may you spend millions of years, you who love Thebes, sitting with your face to the north wind, your eyes beholding happiness." (This was inscribed on the alabaster cup of Tutankhamen.)

FAMILY
Akhenaten, father of Tutankhamen, and Nefertiti, together with three of their daughters. Nefertiti is represented — unusually — as the same size as the Pharaoh, which highlights her importance.

has paintings on the walls. The north wall of the room is covered with a mural that depicts — from right to left — different stages of the journey of the Pharaoh's soul into the world of the Afterlife.

1 **RESURRECTION**
Tutankhamen's successor, the priest Ay, performs the ritual of opening the mouth of the deceased Pharaoh (represented as Osiris, king

of the dead). The ceremony animates the king's mouth, allowing him to speak and breathe, which makes it possible to revive him in the Beyond.

2 **DEIFICATION**
Tutankhamen, as he was in life (signifies that he has returned to be reborn), is received by Nut, Goddess of the Sky,

A narrow room

The four shrines that surrounded the sarcophagus of Tutankhamen like Chinese boxes occupied almost the entire chamber. Carter stated that the space between them and the walls was barely 60 cm (23.6 in), while the roof nearly reached the ceiling. The style of the paintings on the walls is inferior to that in other royal tombs.

1

The young Pharaoh carries the ankh, emblem of eternal life and attribute of divinity, in his hands.

3 **AFTERLIFE**
Adorned with his *nemes* (the headgear that identified him as a Pharaoh), Tutankhamen is received with a welcoming embrace by

Osiris in the world of the dead. Behind the Pharaoh is his *ka*, or essential spirit, in the form of a lookalike.

What Is the Curse of Tutankhamen?

The discovery of the tomb unleashed a storm of apparent omens. It had been said that those who violated the tombs would be punished for this sacrilege. The string of deaths in the following years fueled the notion of the curse.

A mosquito bite on the face, the resulting small abscess cut while shaving, and a subsequent fatal infection led to the death of Lord Carnarvon on April 5, 1923. The cause was officially reported to be pneumonia. No time was lost in publishing the bombshell news in the press with a title that gave everyone something to talk about: "The Revenge of the Pharaoh."

The German lexicographer Adolf Erman, who discovered a grammatical order to Egyptian hieroglyphics, had translated a passage found in the tomb of a noble from the Sixth Dynasty in 1892. It read as follows: "To any who enters this tomb to make it his burial possession, I will capture you as if you were a wild bird and the great god will judge you for it." Such a formula for protection was directed more to one aspiring to the Beyond than to the living searching for treasure. But it also sentenced damnation on those who attempted to take something.

MYSTERIOUS DEATHS

An increasing number of deaths were attributed by the press to the deceased having been "cursed." Not even Lord Carnarvon's dog, said to have died in the family castle in England at the same time as her master, was spared connection with the Pharaoh's curse. It didn't matter that Howard Carter argued against what he called "ridiculous tales." A story was told about a giant cobra (symbol of the millennium and ancient Egypt) that had devoured Carter's canary when he entered the tomb of Tutankhamen, and this was of course associated with the curse.

The spectacular discoveries being made were matched by the spectacular headlines in some newspapers. Word went out that there was a curse written on the walls of the tomb that asserted that "death shall come on swift wings to him who disturbs the peace of the Pharaoh." While this curse has been repeated to this day, the incantation has not been found on any part of the tomb. Although believers in the supernatural highlighted the series of deaths of participants in the enterprise, Egyptologist Herbert Winlock refuted these arguments in 1934, showing that the number of deaths was not statistically greater than in similar expeditions in other environments.

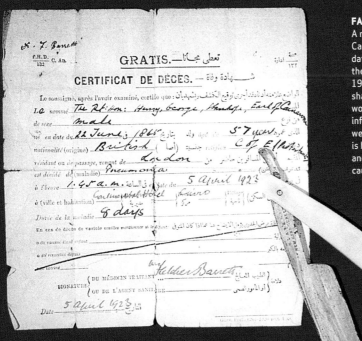

FATAL MOSQUITO BITE
A mosquito bit Lord Carnarvon around the date on which he entered the tomb, November 26, 1922. The next day, while shaving, he opened the wound and it became infected. He died six weeks later. On the left is his death certificate and the blade that caused the infection.

enigmas

Did Tutankhamen Die with Matching Marks?

Lord Carnarvon was bitten on the cheek by a mosquito, which became infected and appears to have caused his death in Cairo. Although this gave rise to numerous unfounded rumors, what is certain is that two years after Carnarvon's death, when the mummy was examined and the bandages removed, a mysterious mark was found on Tutankhamen's left cheek, in the same spot as Lord Carnarvon's wound.

The Curse in the Press

The curse of Tutankhamen was no stranger to the information monopoly. Lord Carnarvon sold an exclusive story regarding Tutankhamen's tomb to the London Times. This stirred up ill will among the rest of the international press, especially the *Daily Mail*, which wanted to pay for the story. The desire for a "scoop" and the "yellow journalism" that prevailed through the early 1980s led to the formation of a list of around thirty supposedly curse-related deaths. Carnarvon was the primary object of the sensational and scandalous exclusives, because his death was in such close proximity to the events, and because he was a renowned figure in British aristocracy. Along with the simultaneous death of his dog, it was notes that, at the time of his death in Cairo, there was a blackout in the city (though this was something that occurred frequently at that time). All these were unverifiable and most likely sensationalist rumors, although there are some persistent enigmas (see column on right), that some refuse to classify as coincidences. It didn't matter to most that Carter made persistent efforts to demystify the esoteric gossip: "The Egyptian funeral ritual did not contain any curse against the living," he stated on more than one occasion. But believers in threatening dark forces from the past millennium remain convinced of the reality of these curses.

Arthur Conan Doyle
1859–1930

The creator of Sherlock Holmes, the most rational detective in literature, was, paradoxically, a firm spiritualist. According to his interpretation, the curse had been caused by mysterious "elementals" created by the priests of the young king.

Marie Corelli
1855–1924

The most popular British novelist at the beginning of the twentieth century participated in propagating the myth: two weeks before the death of Lord Carnarvon, she published a fictional letter where she stated that the "most horrible punishment" awaited those who violated the sealed tomb.

Walter Hauser
1893–1959

The American architect who drew the floor plan of the tomb is one of the strongest pieces of evidence against the supposed curse. He died 37 years after the tomb was opened. His partner, Lindsley Foot Hall (10 years older than Hauser) died even later, in 1969.

What Caused His Death?

The first medical examinations conducted on the mummy of the Pharaoh, by means of autopsy and X-rays, shed some light on his life and death. The 2005 tomography dispelled outstanding doubts, dismissing the theory that he was murdered.

T he first earthly journey of the mummy of Tutankhamen was to the doors of the tomb of Seti II, on the morning of November 11, 1925. The objective: to study the appearance of the embalmed king, uncovering his mortal remains. In the passageway that served as a laboratory for Carter's team, the odyssey began by removing most of the linen bandages covered with jewels, amulets, ointments, and resins. The linens were adhered tightly to the body, and the wrapped body to the mask. The cleaning operation caused serious damage to the mummy, and it was severely mutilated. The autopsy was handled by English anatomist Douglas Derry, a professor at the University of Cairo. Many incisions had to be made, to cut the trunk down the middle, and to remove the arms

and legs. The conclusion was reached that Tutankhamen was between 17 and 19 years old, and 1.67 meters (5 ft 6 in) tall. Despite the carbonized appearance of the head, Carter made the poetic note: "face of an adolescent, noble, with beautiful features ..."

NEW STUDIES

In 1968, Ronald G. Harrison, anatomist from the University of Liverpool, X-rayed Tutankhamen inside his tomb. He found a fragment of bone and a dark mark inside the skull. That possible fracture gave rise to the theory of murder, much more intriguing than accidental death.
Ten years later, Doctor J. E. Harris, from the University of Michigan, performed another X-ray examination to observe the condition of Tutankhamen's teeth. On January 5, 2005, an Egyptian national team under the direction of archaeologist Zahi Hawass,

director of the Supreme Council of Antiquities of Cairo, scanned the mummy for 15 minutes using a portable CAT scan device which was set up beside the tomb. The group of Egyptian scientists worked with the trio that had researched the Ötzi mummy, the Alpine "Iceman" dated as 5,300 years old–Frank Rühli, anatomist from the University of Zurich; Edward Egarter, forensic pathologist from the Archaeological Museum of the Southern Tirol; and Paul Göstner, radiologist from the Bolzano General Hospital. After looking at the 1,700 images taken, they unanimously rejected the murder Hypotheses.
The DNA studies made public in 2010 show that Tutankhamen had a bone disease, and that he had also suffered from malaria (plants to alleviate the fever were found in the tomb), a combination that proved fatal to the Pharaoh.

Bone fragments in the skull

The condition of Tut-ankhamen, with a distressing pattern of bone fractures and tissue wounds, made it difficult to establish what had caused his death. According to Swiss anatomist Frank Rühli, the anatomist who participated in the CAT scan, they would only gain more indications of presumed illnesses and causes of death by means of another tomography of the viscera and of his biological relatives, which for ethical reasons he did not recommend. Generally, it appears the Pharaoh enjoyed a healthy life. Regarding the presence of two bone fragments in the cranial cavity, one of which had already been detected in the 1968 X-ray, the team of scientists in 2005 established that it resulted from a fracture of the first cervical vertebra and the foramen magnum. And he believed there were two possible causes: the embalmers, or Howard Carter's team. The team suspected the same regarding to the absence of the sternum and a large section of the front ribs, which were cleanly cut using a sharp instrument. For some, there will always be doubt as to whether some of the damage could have been caused while the Pharaoh was alive.

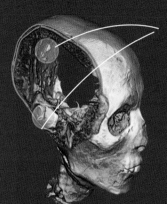

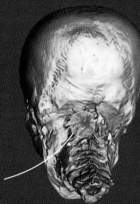

LOOSE BONES
The tomography clearly showed two bone fragments inside the skull, originating from the breakage of a vertebra and the foramen magnum.

HOLE
Observed at the nape of the neck, not the result of a blow, but an orifice made by those responsible for removing the brain in order to mummify the body.

The fracture

The tomography performed on the mummy showed that it had a fracture in the lower part of the left femur. Some scientists believed that it was caused by the Carter team when they removed the mummy from the sarcophagus. Others saw it as the cause of death of the Pharaoh–an open wound that had not healed properly, became infected, and caused his premature death. But the embalmers are still potentially to blame.

ZAHI HAWASS
The Egyptologist supervised the tomography in 2005.

ACCIDENT Some think it is possible that a hunting accident caused the fracture. This mural shows the Pharaoh hunting.

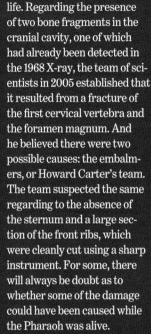

ANKHESENAMUN
The queen and premature widow was one of the most prominent figures at the funeral procession. At the time of Tutankhamen's death, she was about 25 years old. It is known that she placed flowers on the mummy just before the coffins were sealed, and these were still visible when Carter opened the sarcophagus. Later, she married Ay.

CANOPIC SHRINE
The viscera were transferred in this. The brain was extracted through the nose and discarded as having no value.

AY
The adviser and successor of Tutankhamen officiated as head priest and led the pilgrimage to Tutankhamen's final resting place.

THE FUNERAL CORTEGE

The procession was led by the successor to the Pharaoh, Ay, followed by members of the royal family, then the army generals and the high dignitaries of the court. The procession departed from the temple of the city of Thebes (capital of the empire) and ended at the Valley of the Kings, on the other side of the Nile. Despite the enormous procession, the specific location of the tomb was kept completely secret, to protect it from potential thieves.

THE MOURNERS

A group of women who surrounded the main group, crying and lamenting the death of the Pharaoh, were part of the ceremony.

THE SARCOPHAGUS

The mummy was transported inside the sarcophagus. Once inside the tomb, it was removed so as to perform the last rites (such as opening the mouth) before being laid to rest in the burial chamber.

SERVANTS AND SLAVES

They carried the supplies for the tomb, and hauled the sarcophagus and the canopic shrine.

Did the Boy King Really Govern?

The reign of Tutankhamen was established with the Grand Vizier Ay and the Commander of the Army Horemheb directly under him. They were rivals, yet together they held the reins of government. After his death, they successively occupied the post of Pharaoh.

I n the eighth year of the reign of Akhenaten, the "living image of Aten" was born: Tutankhaten, later Tutankhamen. They were times of reform in the eighteenth dynasty of the New Kingdom. The son of Amenhotep III (1390–1353 BCE) and his great royal wife Tiye changed his name from Amenhotep IV to Akhenaten during the fifth year of his reign. He proclaimed the advent of a singular god, Aten, and in so doing removed the hold of power that Amun, other traditional divinities, and especially the clergy (now dedicated

to the worship of Aten) had held. Akhenaten had six daughters with his chief wife Nefertiti, considered the "most beautiful queen in the history of Egypt." Tutankhaten was conceived through his relationship with one of his sisters. A secondary wife, Kiya, has been considered the most likely candidate as the mother of Tutankhamen, but now appears to be excluded (in light of the most recent DNA examinations), since she is not considered a sister of Akhenaten. Around 1332 BCE, the son of Akhenaten was proclaimed Pharaoh under the name Tutankhaten (1332–1323 BCE). He was a

child of eight or nine years who was left to be raised by the two most powerful men of that time: the Grand Vizier Ay and the Commander of the Army Horemheb. Tutankhaten married the third daughter of Akhenaten and Nefertiti, Ankhesenamen, eight years his elder. It was a marriage between half siblings that resulted in two female fetuses in the tomb of Tutankhamen, stillborn descendants of the royal couple.

THE RESTORATION
With the demise of Akhenaten, as of the fourth year the young Pharaoh felt obligated to res-

Relatives and enemies

AMENHOTEP III
1390–1353 BCE
Father of Akhenaten.
Governed for 39 years
in great splendor.

QUEEN TIYE
1390–1340 BCE
Wife of Amenhotep
III and mother of
Akhenaten.

AKHENATEN
1353–1336 BCE
Father of Tutankhamen,
made great religious
reforms.

QUEEN NEFERTITI
1352–1340 BCE
Wife of Akhenaten,
came to govern as
co-regent.

KIYA
Circa 1350 BCE
Second wife of
Akhenaten, with dis-
puted ascendency.

Ay, adviser to three pharaohs

In the reformist times of Akhenaten, Ay, probably the brother of queen Tiye, was married to Tey, better known as Nefertiti's wet nurse. His title of "Father of the God" could be translated as father-in-law of Akhenaten, and he was a fervent follower of Atenism. During the reign of Tutankhamen, he had great power and became the "Divine father." As Grand Vizier, he presided over the funeral honors of the young king and married his widow so that he could legitimately ascend to the Pharaoh's throne, where he spent four years. He did not have descendants, and was succeeded by General Horemheb, the last Pharaoh of the eighteenth dynasty.

tore the worship of Amun and the other gods. He came to be known as Tutankhamen. Memphis became the political capital, and Thebes the religious center. Internal religious harmony and external diplomatic equilibrium were the most notable aspects of his reign. In what is known as the "Restoration Stela," it reads: "Now the gods and goddesses rejoice, the priests are congratulated, the provinces are delighted, and happiness fills the land because good has returned."
However, after his death, nearly all signs of his reign would be erased.

ANKHESENAMUN
1333–1319? BCE
Daughter of Akhenaten and Nefertiti, wife of Tutankhamen.

HOREMHEB
1319–1292 BCE
Succeeded Ay and erased him from the records, along with Akhenaten and Tutankhamen.

Dates indicate the period of their reign.

The pharaoh's physiognomy

A team of archaeologists led by Egyptologist Zahi Hawass examined the results of a computed tomography (CT) scan of the mummy in early 2005. This provided further insights regarding the Pharaoh's physiognomy, along with dispelling doubts about his mysterious death and providing other details about his life.

Advanced technology

In 1972, 50 years after the great discovery by Howard Carter, medicine witnessed one of the greatest advances of all time in the field of radiology: the birth of computed tomography (which in 1979 won its inventors the Nobel Prize in Medicine). Tomography, in existence since the 1930s, is a diagnostic system that, instead of taking a single X-ray image (as conventional radiography does), takes several, and as a result provides a cross-sectional image of a body part. In 1972 a scanner was invented to do the job digitally and process it with a computer. In 1996, the volume generation technique was created to obtain 3D images. This is the technology that was used in early 2005 to examine the tomb of the unfortunate Tutankhamen. The scan only took 15 minutes but the analysis took several months. The mummy had already been X-rayed twice: first in 1968 and then in 1978. This new technique for medical diagnosis, designed to prevent and treat ailments in living patients, proved to be an invaluable tool for bringing the past to life and unveiling one of the most persistent mysteries in history.

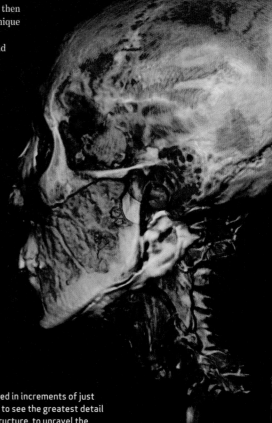

THE SKULL IN DETAIL
The king's head was scanned in increments of just 0.62 mm (0.02 in) in order to see the greatest detail possible of its complex structure, to unravel the mystery of his death and determine whether he suffered from congenital disorders, among other information.

The color of his skin

While science has provided the chance to continually move closer to understanding the distant past, some limits have not yet been overcome. The Pharaoh's skin color will probably always remain unknown to us. Restorers based the reconstruction on paintings and busts of Tutankhamen (left), as well as those of his close relatives. The skin tones of the current Egyptian population were also used as a reference and a intermediate tone from among these was selected.

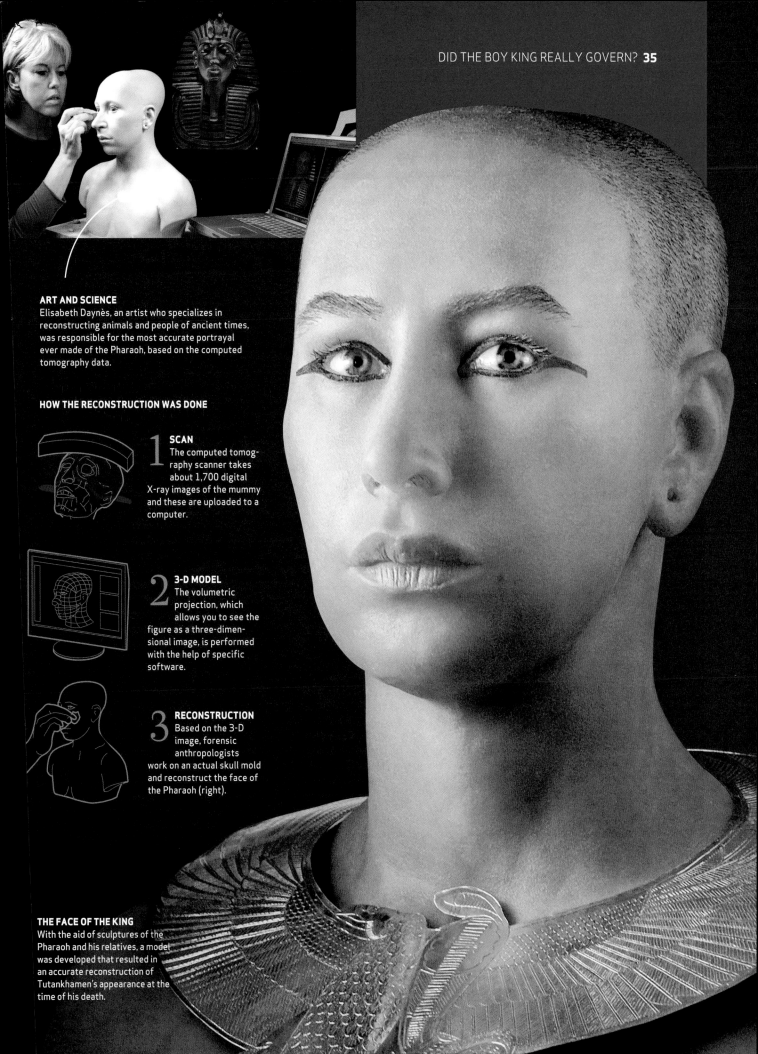

ART AND SCIENCE

Elisabeth Daynès, an artist who specializes in reconstructing animals and people of ancient times, was responsible for the most accurate portrayal ever made of the Pharaoh, based on the computed tomography data.

HOW THE RECONSTRUCTION WAS DONE

1 SCAN
The computed tomography scanner takes about 1,700 digital X-ray images of the mummy and these are uploaded to a computer.

2 3-D MODEL
The volumetric projection, which allows you to see the figure as a three-dimensional image, is performed with the help of specific software.

3 RECONSTRUCTION
Based on the 3-D image, forensic anthropologists work on an actual skull mold and reconstruct the face of the Pharaoh (right).

THE FACE OF THE KING
With the aid of sculptures of the Pharaoh and his relatives, a model was developed that resulted in an accurate reconstruction of Tutankhamen's appearance at the time of his death.

What Rituals Accompanied Mummification?

The process of embalming the Pharaoh's remains was long, complex, and delicate. Everything was done within a careful ritual framework to ensure the survival of the deceased king in the next world, where he would continue his life.

For a firsthand account of the mummification ritual, we turn to Herodotus (484?–425? BCE), Father of History. Book II of his *History* shows that there were three ways to keep dead bodies from rotting. The most comprehensive and difficult, traditionally done for pharaohs and noblemen, was as follows: "They take a piece of twisted iron and with it remove the brain through the nostrils, getting rid of a part of it, while the rest of the skull is cleaned using drugs. Then they make a cut on the side of the torso with a sharp Ethiopian stone and extract the entire contents of the abdomen, which they clean by washing thoroughly with palm wine and an infusion of ground spices. They proceed to fill the cavity with the purest finely ground myrrh, cinnamon, and other spices, with the exception of frankincense, and they stitch up the incision. Finally, they cover the body in natron for seventy days."

He wrote the following about the other two methods of mummification: "If it is desirable to reduce costs by selecting the second procedure, tubes are filled with cedar oil and injected into the abdomen without any cutting or removal of the stomach. The places where liquid could seep out are plugged and the body is placed in natron for the prescribed number of days. After this time, the cedar oil is given an outlet, and it is so potent that it brings with it the liquefied stomach and intestines. Natron, meanwhile, dissolves the flesh and nothing remains of the corpse but the skin and bones. The third method, used in the cases of the poorest people, consists of cleansing the bowels with a laxative and leaving the body in natron for seventy days."

OILS AND RESINS

Once Tutankhamen's corpse became a mummy, his nostrils and lips were plugged with resin. The dessicated body was smeared with oils, waxes, and other odorous and pasty substances. Then began the lengthy process of wrapping the mummy with linen bandages which the embalmer covered with a resinous substance. A priest placed jewels, amulets, and other auspicious ornaments on the mummy — a total of 150 objects. At the end of the process, the mask of solid gold, inlaid with glass paste and semiprecious stones, was placed on the face of the mummy.

Magic in the chamber

The magic of the Afterlife was depicted in the murals discovered on the walls of the burial chamber of Tutankhamen. The craftsmen who were in charge of building and decorating the tombs of the Pharaohs used a unique style that differed from the predominant style of the Akhenaten era. Instead of showing figures in movement, they returned to the more rigid standards of earlier times. On the east wall, facing the treasure room, appears the shrine with the sarcophagus of Tutankhamen on a ship's berth, behind twelve high dignitaries of the kingdom that were carrying him to the Afterlife. It was the first representation of a scene from the "Book of the Dead" in a royal tomb. On the west wall, twelve sitting baboons joyfully receive the boat with two images of Osiris and with a scarab, the symbol of the sun and of regeneration. The most important ceremony of the funeral ritual was captured in the mural on the north wall: the opening of the mouth of the Pharaoh, allowing him to move his lips to speak and eat in the Afterworld. The ritual was performed by the Grand Vizier and successor to the throne, Ay. Spells that were part of the ritual gave rise, many millennia later, to the belief that mummies–roused by mysterious spells–came back to life, a tradition that film took upon itself to showcase repeatedly. One of these prayers says: "Wake up! May you be alert like a living being, rejuvenated every day, healthy from millions of occasions of good sleep, while the gods protect you, with protection around you every day."

enigmas

To whom did the second sarcophagus belong?

The Pharaoh's mummy was protected by the famous burial mask and three nested sarcophagi. The inner sarcophagus is pure gold and weighs about 110 kg (242 lbs). The others are made of wood, covered with sheets of gold. The second coffin (below) is striking at first glance: it looks distinctly different from other representations of Tutankhamen. It is believed that this coffin was originally intended for a predecessor of the young king, but it is unclear who this person was.

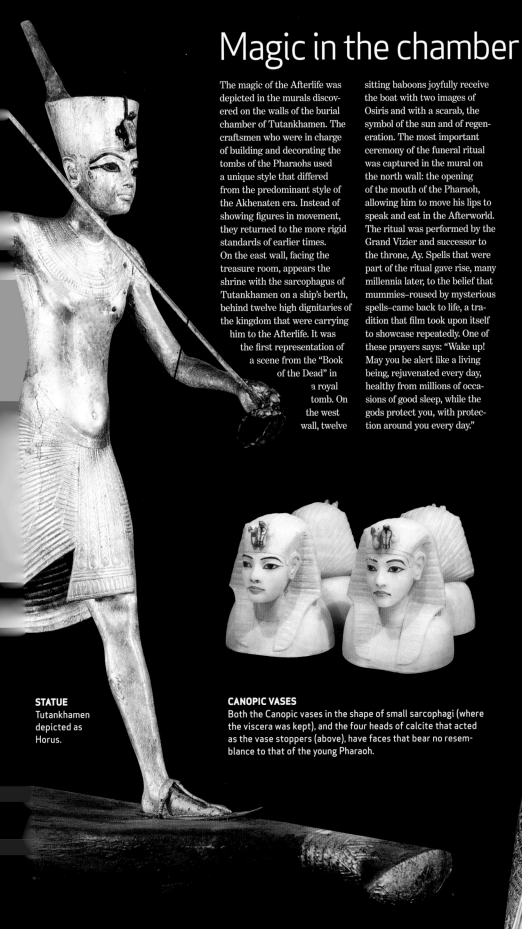

STATUE
Tutankhamen depicted as Horus.

CANOPIC VASES
Both the Canopic vases in the shape of small sarcophagi (where the viscera was kept), and the four heads of calcite that acted as the vase stoppers (above), have faces that bear no resemblance to that of the young Pharaoh.

THE CANOPIC SHRINE

The four internal organs (liver, lungs, stomach, and intestines), which were extracted during embalming were put under the protection of four goddesses: Isis, Nephthys, Neith, and Selkis. A set of four small golden coffins with the internal organs were placed in the four chambers of an alabaster chest, situated inside a shrine surrounded by the four protective goddesses and a frieze of king cobras on top. Across from this magnificent shrine (called the Canopic Shrine), inside the treasure chamber, there was a portable wooden litter in the form of an altar, encrusted in gilded gold, silver, quartz, and obsidian, with Tutankhamen in the form of the seated jackal god Anubis as a sentinel, covered with a linen cloth. Inside the coffin were jewelry, breastplates, amulets, and alabaster vases used in the funeral ceremony. For his journey through the Afterlife, Tutankhamen was provided with a fleet of 35 ships in miniature, modeling the real ships of his time. It was assumed that these models, "activated" by magic, would transport the deceased through the waters of the underworld to then join

with the ship of the sun god, Ra. The scene is represented in murals within the tomb. Here the ushebti ("those who respond"), whose mission was to perform manual tasks on behalf of Tutankhamen in the afterlife, were also represented as small wooden figures overlaid with gold. No less than 413 *ushebti* worked from sunrise to sunset: 365 for each day of the year, 36 foremen in charge of groups of 10 men, and 12 monthly supervisors. However there were no "ostraca," limestone sherds on which matters of daily life were recorded, such as workers' wages.

The furnishings of the tomb revealed the preferences and regular activities of the young king. Images of the Pharaoh in a chariot drawn by two feathered horses during a royal hunt for ostriches appear on a sort of gilded wooden fan, without the original feathers. Bows, arrows, maces, daggers, boomerangs, and spears highlighted the image of Tutankhamen the hunter and warrior of the Afterlife. Another noteworthy image is that of him in the form of Horus on a boat. The table game Senet was another of his favorite pastimes. In the tomb

were four panels of ebony and ivory, each double-sided, mounted on a table with legs of a feline appearance so that he could continue to play in the Afterlife. The game board had 30 squares, in three rows of 10. There

ANUBIS
After immersing the body in natron, the viscera were extracted. Finally, they proceeded to wrap the body. At this stage, the lector priest ("controller of the mysteries") was dressed as Anubis, the god of embalming.

COMING BACK TO LIFE
Hathor, the goddess of the West, "where the sun sets," receives the dead king and revives him by bringing an ankh close to his nose.

Behind the Pharaoh is the god Anubis. The mural is located on the south wall of the room of the sarcophagus in the tomb of Tutankhamen.

are 20 squares on the reverse side of some boards. Known as "the passage," the game represented a trial by fire to gain access to the Afterlife.

In addition to all these treasures, Carter was deeply impressed by what he found on top of the mask of Tutankhamen: a bouquet of delicate flowers was hung around his neck. "That little wreath," he wrote, "was the last farewell offering of the young widow to her husband. All the shining gold was pale against the poor withered flowers, which still retained the dull embodiment of their original colors."

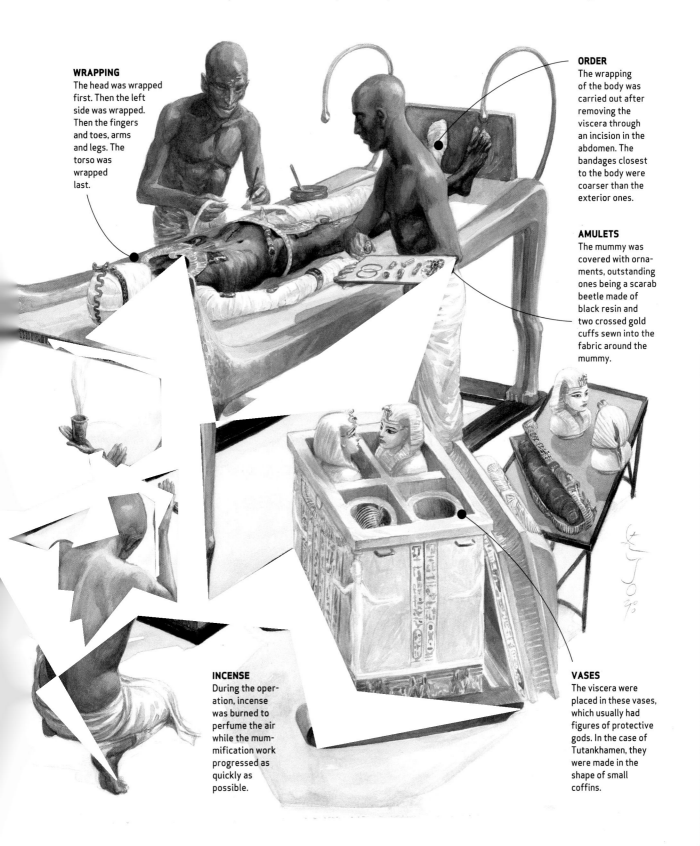

WRAPPING
The head was wrapped first. Then the left side was wrapped. Then the fingers and toes, arms and legs. The torso was wrapped last.

ORDER
The wrapping of the body was carried out after removing the viscera through an incision in the abdomen. The bandages closest to the body were coarser than the exterior ones.

AMULETS
The mummy was covered with ornaments, outstanding ones being a scarab beetle made of black resin and two crossed gold cuffs sewn into the fabric around the mummy.

INCENSE
During the operation, incense was burned to perfume the air while the mummification work progressed as quickly as possible.

VASES
The viscera were placed in these vases, which usually had figures of protective gods. In the case of Tutankhamen, they were made in the shape of small coffins.

Who Desecrated the Tomb of the Pharaoh?

Although it has been often repeated that the tomb of Tutankhamen is the only one found intact, this is not accurate. Shortly after the funeral it was looted twice. There were no visible signs of robbery at the tomb, however.

I n the Valley of the Kings of ancient Thebes, known today as Luxor, 63 royal tombs were discovered. Only one of these, that of Tutankhamen, appeared to be spared from complete looting. In the Ramesside period, the ancient bureaucracy could not keep up with interrogating detained thieves or carrying out inspections of the tombs in order to observe their condition. Many of the dreaded curses that appear on the walls of tombs or on funerary objects were intended to deter the occasional tomb raiders. Given the pillage suffered by the resting places of the Pharaohs, their effectiveness appears to have been minimal.

RADICAL CHANGES

At long last, thanks to the initiative of Pinedjem I (1054–1032 BCE) the tombs were vacated and the mummies buried in ordinary hiding places. Those who entered the tomb of Tutankhamen shortly after his death did so, in Carter's opinion, on at least in two occasions before the doors were permanently sealed by the Theban administration. The seal is unmistakable: the jackal Anubis, guide to the Afterlife, above nine bound enemies, symbols of thieves and evil. The nobleman Maya, supervisor of the treasures in the necropolis and organizer of the funeral of the Pharaoh, might have been the one to re-seal the tomb. It has been suspected that the robbers were members of the funeral cortege.

Seeing what wonderful treasures are contained in the small tomb of a young king such as Tutankhamen, we can only imagine what treasure the great tombs of Pharaohs with more history and influence must have held.

RED-HANDED
This handkerchief, wrapped around eight rings, seems to point to an interrupted robbery.

INTACT
Photograph of the seal of the third tomb, with the rope intact, showing that it had not been entered after the funeral.

Coveted objects

A few weeks after the burial, the tomb robbers quickly sprung into action. Along with jewelry and other precious objects, there were perfumes, ointments, cosmetics, and wine that would all go bad over time. The raiders of Tutankhamen's tomb left their traces in the entryway itself: fragments of gold, vase stoppers, gold-covered wood chips, a bronze arrowhead, knives, a fastener of gilt bronze and among the rubble, some material from the antechamber. Apparently the first group of thieves were interested in metals and were only active in the antechamber and the annex, where everything was in disorder.

The second group went through the whole tomb, but their focus was the royal jewels: about 60 % of the jewelry disappeared, along with metal goblets. Howard Carter concluded that "the thieves were caught inside the tomb or during their escape, perhaps detained with some of the spoils in their possession."

Traces of theft

Although it is often said that the tomb of Tutankhamen is the only one that was found intact, that has proven not to be so. Clear traces of two robberies have been found. The tomb of the pharaoh, fortunately, remained intact through both events, although the second group of thieves reached as far as the burial chamber. The graph on the right shows the various openings that were made by the looters when carrying out the robberies. Some were sealed and others were not. The repair work appears to have been as hasty and careless as that of the thieves. Carter found a mess of piled up objects with no apparent sense of order in the different rooms.

ORIGINAL WALLS
The drawings show the holes made by thieves each time the city was plundered.

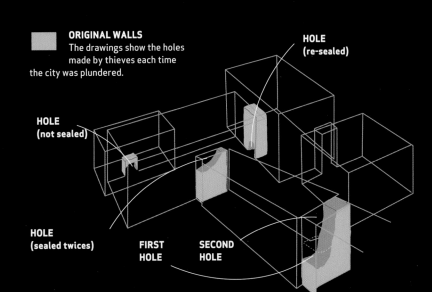

HOLE
(re-sealed)

HOLE
(not sealed)

HOLE
(sealed twices)

FIRST
HOLE

SECOND
HOLE

The Treasure of the Pharaoh

The objects found in the various chambers of Tutankhamen's tomb have untold archaeological value. They are also a treasury of artistic value and richness that may never by equaled among discoveries of historic civilizations.

The mask

The mummy of the Pharaoh was found inside four shrines, a sar-cophagus, and three nested coffins. The mummy was covered by a carefully crafted mask of pure gold with inlays of blue glass and semiprecious stones. It is currently kept in the Egyptian Museum of Cairo and its beauty still awes visitors from around the world. The mask is 54 cm (1 ft, 9.26 in) tall and weighs a little more than 10 kg (22 lbs). The forehead of the likeness of the monarch is adorned with a vulture and a cobra, emblematic gods of Upper and Lower Egypt, respectively. The mask, with the royal striped headdress and a fine braided beard, represents Tutankhamen in the form of Osiris, God of the Dead. While the mask is the most recognizable adornment of the mummy, 150 ornaments were found on the body when it was discovered.

FAN
There were eight fans among the objects found in the tomb. The one in the image has inlays of ebony and a thick gold coating. It is decorated with glass and calcite. There are two cartridges with the names of Tutankhamen in the middle. The feathers did not withstand the passing of time, although they are surprisingly intact on one of the other fans.

The Gold Throne

Six chairs were found among the tomb's furnishings. The most impressive is the Gold Throne, a very elaborate seat with armrests plated with silver and gold. The feet are shaped like those of a lion (there are also ornamental lion heads where the legs meet the armrests) while the side panels have the shape of winged cobras. A scene of Tutankhamen and his wife is depicted on the back.

CROWN
The royal crown, profusely decorated, was found on the head of the mummy. It is made of gold with inlays of stone. The cobra and vulture decorations are removable and were found underneath the body.

VASES
There were around 80 vases in the tomb. Their strange shapes fascinated Carter. The one in the image is a calcite drinking cup in the shape of a lotus flower.

FIGURINES
Small gold-covered wooden sculptures that represent the Pharaoh, part of a set of 32. They are 85 cm (2 ft 9.46 in) tall and have primarily ritual value.

ANUBIS
Tutankhamen, in the form of the god Anubis, the god of embalming. The figure, carved in wood and varnished with black resin, rests on a coffin that contained ritual objects.

Alternative Hypotheses

Who was Tutankhamen's father?

In February 2010, the results of DNA tests on several mummies related to Tutankhamen were made public, and it could be established with certainty that mummy KV55 was Tutankhamen's father. However, the identity of this mummy, discovered in 1907 by Theodore M. Davis, continues to be controversial. For decades, the majority of archaeologists considered the mummy to be that of Akhenaten, and Zahi Hawass himself favored this Hypotheses. However, there are inconsistencies in the DNA of this mummy in relation to the fetuses in Tutankhamen's tomb (considered to be his descendants), and so some think that it may belong to the enigmatic Smenkhkare.

Was Akhenaten Moses?

The Pharaoh Akhenaten began daring religious reform, proclaiming that Aten–the sun disk–was the "only god," substituting him for Amun as the main god of the Egyptian pantheon. Although he did not deny the existence of other gods (in fact, he considered himself to be a god), his policy became more and more intolerant toward the cult of Amun. He eventually banned the name of said god, and even deleted the term "gods" from the scriptures. The similarity to Jewish monotheism was noted long ago. Sigmund Freud had ventured that Moses may have been an Egyptian noble, a priest of the cult of Amun, who had to escape from Egypt with his followers when Akhenaten died. An Egyptian author, Ahmed Osman, even stated that Moses and Akhenaten were the same person. According to this author, Yuya, Akhenaten's grandfather, was the biblical Joseph (the interpreter of dreams). However, the accepted opinion among experts is that Moses lived during the reign of Ramses II, a century after Akhenaten.

PREDECESSOR AND FATHER?
Bust of Akhenaten that shows (and exaggerates) his elongated face. It is very likely that he was the father of Tutankhamen. Some researchers have speculated that he and Moses could be the same person.

Does the mask emit radiation?

Alternative schools of thought have believed there to be supernatural properties in some of the objects from Ancient Egypt. The diviner Jacques La Maya detected a negative green emission between the crossed arms of the Egyptian statues. Creations such as the "Atlantis Ring" or the ring of Jua (a supposed Egyptian priest) could have the opposite effect of the negative green emission, acting as a protection or talisman for its wearer. The Swiss geobiologist Blanche Merz, on the other hand, measured highly positive radiation in the *uraeus* that crowned Tutankhamen's golden mask.

Who was Pharaoh Smenkhkare?

There was a three-year dark period between the reigns of Akhenaten and Tutankhamen. Archaeological evidence points to a successor of Akhenaten, named Smenkhkare, who would have been coregent for some time and then would have ruled for only three years. He could be the son of Akhenaten but the matter becomes complex because he is sometimes represented as a woman. Also, the time he appears on the scene coincides with the disappearance of Nefertiti, Akhenaten's wife, from the records. Scholars debate whether Smenkhkare is Nefertiti (who would have taken a man's name); or is a son of Akhenaten; or the husband of Meritaten, one of Akhenaten's daughters, who would have survived Smenkhkare and would have succeeded him, which would explain his double appearance as man and woman. There are several combinations among these hypotheses, but little is known for certain. Finding the mummy of Nefertiti–a figure who seems to have had unusual power in the times of Akhenaten, which leads some Egyptologists to think she reached the rank of Pharaoh– would probably clear up many uncertainties.

ENIGMATIC BEAUTY
The imperturbable face of Nefertiti has fascinated humanity for centuries. Her life is a mystery.

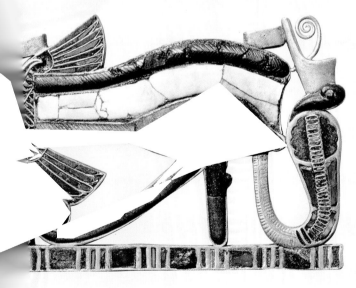

POSITIVE SYMBOL
Pectoral used as a talisman featuring the "Eye of Horus" (or *Udyat*) and the *uraeus* (the upright cobra, symbol of royalty) to its right.

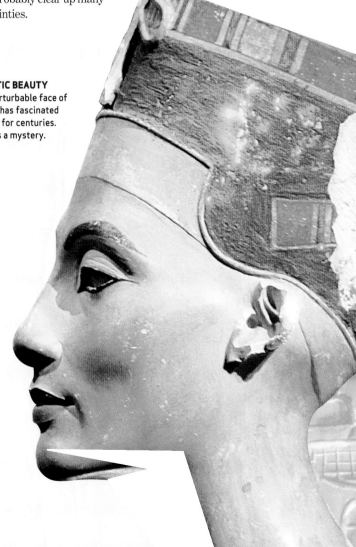

Was the Mummy of the King's Wife Found?

In the tomb of Pharaoh Tut-ankhamen, the mummified bodies of two female fetuses, at around five and seven months of gestation, were found. DNA tests determined that they are the daughters of Tutankhamen and mummy KV21A. It is believed that this mummy could be his wife, Ankhesenamun. While this Hypotheses is very likely (Tut-ankhamen died young, and it is not known that he had another wife), her identity is still in the realm of speculation.

Was the Tomb Constructed According to the Golden Ratio?

Several archaeologists have found that Egyptian architecture has harmonious proportions, according to what is known as the golden ratio. In Tutankhamen's tomb, the Royal Chamber, whose function was to facilitate the rebirth of the monarch, was built according to the golden ratio (1.618); while the antechamber, where any potential intruder would arrive, has an inharmonious proportion (2.222).

Why Was the Valley Chosen as the Royal Cemetery?

Katarin Parizek, a photographer and geologist from Pennsylvania State University, recognized geological structure patterns in the Valley of the Kings. Many of the tombs lie on fracture traces. The passages and chambers in the tombs perfectly align with these geologically weak areas. Parizek suggests that the builders chose these areas because the rocks are easier to excavate. However, researchers in geobiology speculate that they could have taken advantage of electromagnetic effects on the rocks. Also, noxious gases of geological origin, such as the radioactive gas Radon, can seep out from underground through the faults, which would contribute to the theory that the Egyptian tomb curses had a biological basis.

DAUGHTER OF TUTANKHAMEN
Mask that covered one of the small mummies of fetuses found in Tutankhamen's tomb. It is believed that both were the daughters of the Pharaoh and his wife, Ankhesenamun.

How Did the Place of Burial Go Unnoticed?

The reign of Tutankhamen was during a revolutionary period in the history of Ancient Egypt. When the young king took the throne, the worship of Aten, begun by Akhenaten, was active. During the reign of Tutankhamen, Egyptian society returned to ancient tradition, and the worship of Amun was revived, with Amun as the main god of Egypt. Later, Pharaoh Horemheb took official action against all Pharaohs who had been part of religious reform, including Tutankhamen. The Pharaoh, who it seems never came to possess true power, was forgotten, along with Akhenaten and Ay. His tomb was also neglected, and the later tomb of Ramses VI was placed directly on top of Tutankhamen's, further contributing to the lack of awareness of its location. Huts for workers were also set up on top of the tomb in the Ramesside Period. However, while the tombs of Akhenaten and Ay were desecrated and damaged, Tutankhamen's remained virtually untouched. Horemheb respected the young king, perhaps because he recognized that he was a Pharaoh without the capacity to make decisions, or because he had kept him as head of the army during his reign.

Was Tutankhamen Deformed?

For a long time it was thought that the young pharaoh suffered from a congenital disease that may have caused physical deformities, and the busts of the king with an elongated skull and stretched features were cited as an example in support of this theory. His relation to Akhenaten, who is depicted with serious deformities, was also mentioned. While it is thought that these disproportionate figures could be exaggerations that transmitted a symbolic message (sometimes Akhenaten appears with the breasts of a woman or without the virile organ), it was also postulated that both Akhenaten and Tutankhamen suffered from Marfan syndrome or Fröhlich's syndrome. Since the latter implies the inability to produce children (and Akhenaten had several), this Hypotheses was discarded.

STRANGE FEATURES
One of the two life-sized statues of the king that guards the entrance to his tomb. The elongated skull seems to be a family trait.

Experts who examined the mummy in 2005 affirmed that "the oblong shape of his skull–similar to that of other members of his family–was not caused by any illness." This feature, even though exaggerated, is considered to be within the standards of physical normality. Today, it is known that Tutankhamen suffered from Kohler's disease, which, together with malaria (and a fractured leg), caused his death.

To See and Visit

▼ OTHER AREAS OF INTEREST

THEBES
LUXOR, EGYPT

Thebes, the capital of Ancient Egypt during the New Kingdom, was found in what is now Luxor. For this reason, it is considered to be the "world's greatest open air museum." It lies across the river from The Valley of the Kings and includes the colossal ruins of the Karnak and Luxor temples.

NEUES MUSEUM
BERLIN, GERMANY

As of October 2009, the Egyptian Museum of Berlin is located in the Neues Museum. It has a collection of very high historical value whose objects include the bust of Nefertiti, as well as other works of art from the period of Tutankhamen.

EGYPTIAN MUSEUM OF CAIRO
CAIRO, EGYPT

This is the most significant museum of Egyptian culture in the world. The museum houses the treasures of Tutankhamen's tomb, except for the mummy itself, which is found in the original tomb in The Valley of the Kings. Of the 120,000 objects in the museum (including 27 royal mummies), Tutankhamen's burial mask is the most appreciated by visitors.

EXHIBITS IN THE OLD WORLD
EUROPE

"Tutankhamen: His Tomb and His Treasures" is an exhibit that has been on display for two years in European cities, with high quality replicas of objects from the Pharaoh's tomb. The exhibit will continue traveling throughout the continent.

The Valley of the Kings

SECTORS
The necropolis of the ancient Egyptian capital, Thebes, is found around 435 miles (700 km) from Cairo. The tomb of Tutankhamen can be visited (for an additional fee) as can those of other pharaohs in the Eastern sector of the Valley. In the Western sector, only the tomb of Ay, Tutankhamen's successor, can be entered, also with a fee.

WEATHER
The valley is in a very hot region. Therefore, it is best to visit in months when the weather is as its best, from October to March. It is recommended to come prepared for rugged terrain and high temperatures: with sunglasses, sunscreen, comfortable and durable footwear, a wide-brimmed hat or baseball cap, and plenty of water. Visitors should bear in mind that the area is a highly-visited tourist site throughout the year.

TOMBS
For the casual visitor, a visit to three or four tombs in the valley can take half a day. Not all of the tombs are open to the public, and those that are, are open during different seasons. Tutankhamen's tomb is very modest. His treasures are found in the Egyptian Museum of Cairo. Therefore it is advisable to visit other more luxurious tombs such as KV9 of Ramses VI or KV11 of Ramses III.

The Valley of the Queens

The Valley of the Queens, where the tombs of queens from the Ramesside Period are found, is very close to the Valley of the Kings. Also nearby, Deir el-Bahari, another burial ground where the magnificent temple of Queen Hatshepsut stands, can be visited.

CITY OF AMARNA
EGYPT
Located 248.5 miles (400 km) to the north of Luxor is the city founded by Akhenaten, who gave it his name. Today it is known as Amarna. Although it was abandoned 15 years after being founded, it has important ruins such as the unfinished tomb of Akhenaten.

MUSEO EGIZIE
TURIN, ITALY
This houses the most substantial collection of Egyptian relics after that on display at the Egyptian Museum of Cairo. The oldest copy of the *Book of the Dead* is among the noted pieces. The statues of Ramses the II and Horemheb, the last Pharaoh of the eighteenth dynasty, are also noteworthy.

THE BRITISH MUSEUM
LONDON, THE UNITED KINGDOM
This museum houses the world's third most significant collection of pieces from Ancient Egypt. The famous Rosetta Stone stands out among the main objects, as do busts of Amenhotep III, Tutankhamen's grandfather. For years the Egyptian authorities have demanded, unsuccessfully, that the Rosetta Stone be returned.

TRAVELING EXHIBIT
NEW YORK, THE UNITED STATES
"Tutankhamen and The Golden Age of the Pharaohs" is an exhibit organized by National Geographic since 2005, with royal objects from the tomb. The exhibit still continues its successful tour around the world.

The Dead Tell Us Their Story

P eople and cultures around the world have developed various ways of dealing with one of the most significant events in life: its end. Death is something no one has been able to avoid and, therefore, is something we all have in common. The ritual treatment of the dead is considered one of the earliest and most fundamental indicators of culture, and the changes this treatment has undergone over time and space have intrigued humanity for millennia. But only in the last few decades has technology advanced to where it allows the dead to tell us so much about their personal stories and, in a sense, to come back to life. Technological methods such as virtual autopsies, 3D modeling, DNA and isotopic analysis and facial reconstruction, to name a few, have been applied with stunning results. Now we are able to find out a good deal about the lives of specific individuals who died without leaving any written clues. This knowledge includes information as significant and diverse as the cause of death, the places where they lived, changes in their diet, what diseases they suffered, how they looked when alive, and their perception of the afterlife.

Much of this information comes from studying mummies, corpses whose skin has been preserved on the skeleton either through natural or artificial processes. And while the vast majority of human remains are not mummies but skeletons, these also provide a large amount of data, which increases when considereing the offerings and other objects found near them.

Human remains stimulate the imagination of millions, as they always have. Mummies have been featured in numerous television documentaries, have attracted large crowds at exhibitions, and never cease to inspire fictional sensation in books and movies. Many children's interest in mummies is surpassed only by their interest in dinosaurs. Their educational potential is extensive, since they can be used as a tool for teaching subjects as diverse as archaeology, geography, human biology, nutrition, health, and environmental conservation.

This book presents examples of burials from all over the world, and that date back several millennia, including mummies that predate those of the Egyptians by more than two thousand years. It focuses on some of the most famous funerary mysteries of the past: the Chinese mausoleum of Qin Shi Huang with its terracotta warriors; the bog bodies of Northern Europe; the Lord of Sipán in northern Peru; the Caucasian mummies in the Tarim basin in western China; and Ötzi the Iceman found in the Italian Alps.

Since low temperatures are one of the best ways to preserve organic matter, frozen tombs provide access to the past in a way that is unattainable by any other means.

The excellently well-preserved frozen mummies provide a unique opportunity for studies in fields as diverse as parasitology, DNA analysis, microbiology, paleopathology, and prehistoric diet. The information obtained from the research on the Alpine Iceman has revolutionized our understanding of Neolithic man. Since technology is constantly evolving, the frozen bodies continue to make new contributions to our knowledge base as new techniques become available. They contain extremely complex information spanning a wide range of scientific disciplines and in the coming years yet more, new data will be obtained, and it will continue to be so as long as humanity exists.

The documentation of human remains as well as the discoveries that are made concerning them, have helped deepen our understanding of cultures from around the world. This has contributed to the preservation of a priceless heritage for future generations to come. Yet more tombs will continue to be discovered, and the documented cases of ancient tombs will never cease to fascinate those who share in humanity's search for meaning in the universe.

JOHAN REINHARD
Archaeologist, mountaineer, and explorer-in-residence of the National Geographic Society. He has discovered and recovered several Inca mummies in the peaks of the Andes. He is the author of *The Ice Maiden: Inca Mummies, Mountain Gods, and Sacred Sites in the Andes* (2005).

VALLEY OF MOCHE
Aerial view of the pyramids
of Sipán, a goldmine among
archaeological sites in the
Americas.

Unveiling the Secrets of Death

If our manner of understanding death says a lot about our lives, then rituals for facing it could be said to define civilizations. Ancient tombs are an open book for archaeologists, but they still hold many mysteries.

Nowadays ancient tombs, beyond being an open book, are almost an entire encyclopedia. Archaeologists, along with coroners, biologists, biochemists, and DNA specialists, are drawing the family tree of the human species from its earliest origins thanks to increasingly precise techniques and methods for preserving and dating the finds. What appear most in archaeological excavations are objects. But when in addition to offerings and ceremonial utensils the intact remains of the deceased are found, the picture changes, and even more so if they are mummified. Mummification, when it is not a result of natural causes (dehydration, freezing, or absence of oxygen, as in peat bogs), is a clear indicator of the existence of a complex and well-structured society, able to include among their funerary rituals techniques for preserving the human body that amaze us to this day.

ANALYSIS OF MUMMIES

Mummies allow us to be face to face with a human being who died thousands of years ago. They also open an authentic window into the past. Science today not only allows us to study and analyze in depth the bones, skin, and DNA of a human body, but also to reconstruct it so that, in addition to knowing the age and gender of a mummy, we can discern its facial features. From the study of the guts, skin and bones, researchers may also know the cause of death, how they spent the last days of their lives, what they ate, and from what diseases they may have suffered or even how many times they suffered serious injuries. However, as we acquire more

and more information, the unknowns also increase exponentially. Most of the time these uncertainties remain unresolved, as is the case of a very interesting and outstanding group of over a hundred mummies that appeared in 1983 in the Chilean Atacama desert, in Chinchorro, near the city of Arica. These were the Chinchorro people, who inhabited the coasts of what is now southern Peru and northern Chile between 9000 and 1500 BCE. They are considered the oldest culture in the Americas. It is known that the Chinchorro people were fishermen who did not practice agriculture and did not use pottery or the loom. They did not leave monuments or texts. The only objects found were some very basic tools and well-crafted shell hooks. However, their spiritual lives, given their unusual mummification techniques must have been complex.

TOMB OF HEROD I
Aerial view of the Herodium, where, according to the historian Josephus (first century), Herod the Great was buried.

The mummies of the Chinchorro culture are peculiar, and were not designed to remain in their graves. Rather, they seem to have been made to be worshiped in rituals, to be placed in public places next to the images of the gods, thereby fulfilling the role of protectors of the community. They are like statues, works of art created with the bodies of the ancestors. They wear masks and wigs made from human hair. Organs were removed and the bodies were also dismembered to later be reassembled and re-covered by the skin, sustained by an internal structure of sticks and reeds, held together with an ash paste. One is about 7,000 years old, 2,000 years older than the most ancient Egyptian mummies. It is believed that the Chinchorro people abandoned the practice of artificial mummification around 1700 BCE. Their successors merely buried their dead in the desert, where many bodies ended up being mummified by natural causes.

Among some pre-Inca cultures as well as the Inca, mummies were considered huacas, powerful beings that provided fertility and good harvests, and connected the natural and the supernatural, the gods and men. Of the Inca mummies found, such as those on Mount Ampato, the most famous is the Inca Ice Maiden: a 14-year-old girl who was probably offered as a sacrifice to the gods on a platform built for the occasion at over 19,685 ft above sea level.

Her corpse must have been frozen around 1466, at the time of the Inca ruler Yupanqui. She was discovered in 1993 by Johan Reinhard, after the eruption of a volcano that thawed the ice that surrounded her, and was given the nickname "Juanita." The mummy, extraordinarily well preserved, has provided invaluable information to historians. The DNA analysis, for example, revealed that her father was a native of a village in Panama.

But Chile and Peru are just two of many places in the world where mummies of great archaeological value have been found.

In Ancient Egypt, mummifying took place for over 30 centuries. Initially, only the Pharaohs and leading members of the priestly class were mummified; then significant people, and in the end, any citizen who could afford it could be mummified, and even animals. Despite the long history of this custom, modern science has never been able to say with certainty what technique the Egyptian embalmers actually used

CHINCHORRO
The mummies of the Chinchorro culture are styled differently, according to their age: they are black, red, or have a patina of clay, like the one shown in the photograph.

NEWGRANGE
This Irish mausoleum is one of the most monumental as well as primitive examples of mound tomb culture, which was common in Europe and Asia in the Bronze Age.

on their mummies. Mummification was an oral tradition, and its secrets were passed on by the best teachers. No text or painting has ever been found where the procedures used were described. While the Greek historian Herodotus gave some clues, they were merely hearsay. Today, science can only surmise how it was carried out. However, in 1994 a mummification process took place in a laboratory in the United States (authorized and consented to, and the only such process documented to date), the outcome of which was considered a success.

NECROPOLIS

The oldest tombs continue to hide ancient mysteries. One of them is the prehistoric necropolis of Brú na Bóinne (Palace of the Boyne, in Irish Gaelic) including the Newgrange passage tomb, in the Boyne River Valley. Newgrange is a monument built by a Mesolithic culture between 3300 and 2900 BCE (500 years before the Great Pyramid of Giza was built). It was discovered in the seventeenth century and excavated between 1962 and 1975. It is a large circular mound covering an area 230 ft in diameter, made with 97 large stones topped by a white quartz and granite wall leaning inward. A 55 ft. passage leads to a cruciform chamber whose roof has remained intact for about 5,000 years and where funerary rituals could have been carried out. Large stone vessels have been found there containing the cremated remains of at least five individuals. The site is aligned with the stars and has a narrow opening of about 4 in above the entrance. One week before and one week after each winter solstice, the sun's rays penetrate that opening and illuminate the gallery all the way to the center of the chamber, where a block of stone decorated with beautiful spirals is located. Some believe that human sacrifices were made here, but generally it is considered to have been the sacred repository of the ashes of important people, who would have been cremated outside. The truth is that besides the age of the site, everything else is conjecture. No one knows

Continued on page 58 ▶

The world of death

Tombs and mummies are very important findings for archaeologists. All around the world, bodies have been discovered and burial sites have been explored that have provided a great wealth of information on extinct civilizations and societies.

Tollund Man
(fourth century BCE)

Normanton Down and Avebury Barrows
(2600-1600 BCE)

Lindow Man
(20 BC-130 CE)

Gallagh Man
(400-200 BCE)

Newgrange
(3100 BCE)

EUROPE

Bougon
(4700 BCE)

La Tène
(seventh-first centuries BCE)

Catacombs of Ro
(first century BCE - sixth century CE)

Menga
(3000 BCE)

Mausoleum of Medracen
(3000 BCE)

Guanche Mummies
(third-fifteenth centuries CE)

Tholos Tombs of Mycenae
(1350 BCE)

NORTH AMERICA

PACIFIC OCEAN

Cahokia Burial Mound 72
(700-1400 CE)

Grave Creek Mound
(250-150 BCE)

Shafts Tombs
(300 BC - 600 CE)

CENTRAL AMERICA

Pakal's Tomb
(675-702 CE)

Tombs

Mummies

Leimebamba
(800-1570 CE)

Tierradentro
(sixth-tenth centuries)

2

Sipán
(100-700 CE)

Inca Mummy "Juanita"
(1450-1530)

Sechin Mummy
(1800-1200 BCE)

SOUTH AMERICA

Paracas
(700 BC - 200 CE)

Chullpas of Sillustani
(1200-1450 CE)

1

Chinchorro
(7020-1500 BCE)

Inca Cave
(4000 BCE)

Llullaillaco
(fifteenth century)

ATLANTIC OCEAN

PACIFIC OCEAN

1 CHINCHORRO

The Chinchorro mummies, found in Arica (Chile), are considered the world's oldest example of embalming.

2 HYPOGEA

The location and construction of the Hypogea of Tierradentro demonstrate the importance of eternal life to that pre-Columbian culture.

ASIA

FIRE AND EARTH

Between the Bronze and Iron ages, Europe saw a radical change in funeral rites. They shifted from burial mounds to cremation. The ashes of the deceased were placed in pots or urns (like the one pictured) and buried in urn fields.

d Ship
E)

hdorf Burial Mound
enth-sixth centuries BCE)

Ötzi the Iceman
(3255 BCE)

Hallstatt
(1000-500 BCE)

Etruscan Necropolis
(seventh-second centuries BCE)

Thracian Tomb of Kazanklak
(fourth century BCE)

Varna
(4500-4000 BCE)

Herod's Tomb
(first century BCE)

qara
7-323 BCE)

Royal Tombs of Ur
(2450-2350 BCE)

Tomb of Cyrus
(540-530 BCE)

of Giza
72 BCE)

Petra
(end of first century BCE-100 CE)

Naqsh-e Rustam
(1000-330 BCE)

the Kings
69 BCE)

Abydos
(3500-100 BCE)

ramids at Meroe
th centuries BCE)

RICA

Kurgan of Pazyryk
(fifth-third centuries BCE)

Cherchen Man
(1000 BCE)

Ming Dynasty Tombs
(1409-1584)

Mancheng
(113-104 BCE)

Tang Tombs
(seventh-tenth centuries)

Mausoleum of Qin Shi Huang
(210 BCE)

Anyang
(thirteenth-eleventh centuries BCE)

Mawangdui
(186-168 BCE)

Lady Dai (Xin Zhui)
(178-145 BCE)

Mounds of the Silla Kings
(350-550)

Nintoku Tomb
(fifth century)

INDIAN OCEAN

PACIFIC OCEAN

3 FUNERAL SHIP

A Viking boat was discovered under a burial mound, perfectly preserved, with the mast, rudder, ropes, and 16 pairs of oars.

4 TUTANKHAMUN

The discovery of the intact tomb of this Pharaoh in the Valley of the Kings was a milestone in the history of Egyptology.

5 NINTOKU'S TOMB

This is the largest burial mound in the world, with a length of (1,600 ft. It is part of the Mozu burial site located in Osaka, known for its keyhole shaped tombs.

for certain which culture erected it, and there are no other known remains of their civilization. All that remains is this unusual Neolithic monument, made of carved stones engraved with spiral, circle, and zigzag patterns, which were hidden under a mountain for 5,000 years.

At the heart of another mountain there are tombs that have not yet revealed their secrets, and which still hold the remains of people who were considered sacred in their time. Some were actually surrounded by a replica of their entire empire for their final voyage. This is the case of the tomb of the first emperor and unifier of China, Qin Shi Huang, whose body, according to his wish, allegedly lies beneath a mountain of earth planted with trees so that he could not be found. The emperor died in 210 BCE, and his immense grave was ignored for about 2,000 years until 1974, when some farmers digging a well discovered some of the thousands of terracotta figures that were buried there, representing his great army.

BURIAL COMPLEXES

For 500 years, the archaeological site Huaca Rajada maintained its role as a burial ground. It has the greatest wealth of any burial complex in the Americas, and was discovered in 1987. The discovery of the tomb of the Lord of Sipán, who rested for centuries along with his ancestors amidst a rich array of funerary goods, has led to a deeper understanding and even a rewriting of the history of America and particularly of the Moche people–a society that developed between the first and seventh centuries in Peru and whose rulers were considered to be demigods.

The royal mausoleum of Sipán was built in the second century AD. It consists of a large adobe platform 394 ft long, 197 ft wide, and 49 ft high, in which several architectural phases have been discerned. So far, nearly 70 tombs have been excavated and their contents are being thoroughly examined to reveal secrets from their past.

A similar case is the tomb of Herod, king of Judea from 37 – 4 BCE, who was buried in Herodium, a fortress-palace that he had built on top of a hill in what is now the West Bank, 7 mi south of Jerusalem. The tomb was discovered in 2007 by archaeologist Ehud Netzer of the Hebrew University of Jerusalem. Although no inscription has been found that corroborates these are the remains of the king, a sarcophagus broken into hundreds of pieces has been found, which could have been his.

THE ICEMAN

Among the messengers from the past who have appeared to reveal some of their secrets, Ötzi the Iceman must be mentioned. He was discovered in the Alps in 1991. He was about 40 years old when he died about 5,300 years ago, and along with him were 74 objects that have given insights into the world in which he lived. Also worth noting are a group of mummies discovered in the late nineteenth century by Aurel Stein in the Tarim Basin in China, which could only be studied as of 1970. They are dated between 4,000 and 2,000 BCE, and have a peculiarity: red hair, tall stature and Caucasian features. Why they were there remains a mystery.

There is also mystery surrounding another large group of mummies known as the "bog bodies." There are over a thousand of them, found in bogs in northern Europe. Some are 2,000 years old, and almost all of them show signs of violent deaths. The list of ancient burial complexes is extensive. Some, like the Valley of the Kings and the Hypogeum of the Pharaoh Tutankhamun in Egypt, the catacombs of Rome, and the royal tombs of Ur, are famous. Additionally, the Moche pyramids, as well as the Etruscan, Mycenaean, Celtic, Chinese, and Japanese burial mounds, and other necropolises or isolated tombs that are less known, pose great challenges to archaeologists and historians.

◀ *Continued from page 55*

Victor Henry Mair
1943

Professor of Chinese studies at the University of Pennsylvania since 1979. He was part of the interdisciplinary team that studied the Caucasian mummies of the Tarim Basin in China. Based on the experience, he wrote the book *The Tarim Mummies: Ancient China and the Mystery of the Earliest Peoples from the West*, which analyzes the role of Central Asia in the human and intercultural interconnections between East and West.

DRIVING FORCE. Although he was a philologist, he took an active role in organizing the project of researching the Tarim mummies.

Johan Reinhard
1943

Born in Illinois and completing his Ph.D. in Anthropology in Vienna, the American explorer is an expert in mountain archaeology. He specializes in researching the villages of the Andes, and has discovered numerous famous mummies on several Andean Peaks.

MOUNTAINEER. His discovery of the mummies in Ampato and Llullaillaco, at high altitude, served to confirm the ritual sacrifice of young Inca.

Walter Alva

This Peruvian archaeologist gained international fame in 1987. After being warned by the police that grave robbers were looting an adobe pyramid in the enclosure of Huaca Rajada, in Sipán, he found a goldmine in the mausoleum of a powerful Moche ruler, given the name of "the Lord of Sipán." This discovery was considered to have revealed the most significant of all pre-Columbian American graves. Alva, director of the Brünning Archaeological Museum of Lambayeque–his home province–and also the modern Museum of the Royal Tombs of Sipán, is an authority on the Moche culture, which flourished between the first and fourth centuries in northern Peru. He has been honored by the Peruvian government for his research, receiving the Order of the Sun (the highest award bestowed by Peru to commend notable civil and military merit). His excavations have helped increase awareness of pre-Inca cultures. In 2007 he discovered the murals of the temple of Ventarrón which date back 4,000 years and are considered the oldest in the Americas.

REVELATION. The discovery of the Lord of Sipán revealed that the pyramids of Huaca Rajada were part of the Moche culture, and not the Chimú culture as was previously believed.

1951

> *"It's an indescribable feeling to know that you are experiencing the dream of every archaeologist, and at the same time you have the responsibility to care for and protect, for posterity, the legacy of your story."*
> *Walter Alva*

Xu Weihong

1966

With a degree in archaeology from the University of Gansu, Xu is the director of the archaeological team that unearthed the famous terracotta warriors. She has been devoted to their preservation since 1989, the year she joined the famous Museum of Xian. Under the direction of Xu Weihong, new sites linked to the mausoleum of Qin Shi Huang have been explored, in which human forms and birds were found, as well as animal skeletons. According to Weihong, archaeological findings seem to confirm the legends about the tomb of the first Chinese emperor. Her work in research and preservation has been internationally recognized.

CAUTIOUS. Fearing that damage could be done to the mythical tomb that lies under the emperor's mound, Xu Weihong's team is waiting until there is technology available that is capable of preserving its contents.

Ehud Netzer
1934–2010

Israeli architect, professor, and tenacious archaeologist, specializing in the architecture of Herod's reign. He began excavations at Herodium in 1972. After 25 years of work, he found Herod's destroyed sarcophagus, identical to that described by Josephus.

DISCOVERER. The finding of the tomb of Herod by Netzer confirmed the veracity of the ancient texts.

The Eighth Wonder

Emperor Qin Shi Huang (260–210 BCE), the first ruler to unify China, left behind a tomb as grand as his legacy. While it was ignored for centuries, an accidental discovery in 1974 gave archaeologists the clue to finding one of the most spectacular treasures of humanity, considered by some the "eighth wonder of the world."

The Grand Mausoleum of the Emperor

The desire for immortality had always plagued Qin Shi Huang. For that reason, shortly after taking the throne, he began building his monumental tomb. With each of his conquests, the number of workers at the site increased until there were 700,000 working toward completing his funerary obsession. After his death, the work was discontinued.

Hidden Pyramid
It is believed that under the earthen mound of the mausoleum there is a hidden pyramid where the emperor's sarcophagus rests. Since the tomb has not been excavated, this rendering is based on the descriptions of Sima Quin, the second century BCE historian.

Bronze Chariots
Two full-scale replicas of bronze chariots were found.

Exterior Wall

345 m

350 m

Site of Civil Servants

Sarcophagus Chamber
According to Sima Quin, the emperor's bronze coffin was laid to rest in a room also made of bronze. The ceiling was painted blue. The floor featured a map showing the establishing of China.

Site of Acrobats

CHRONOLOGY OF FINDINGS

1974	1976	1980	1998	1999	2000
The first pit with terracotta warriors was discovered, 0.74 mi from the mausoleum.	Skeletons of horses buried alive in imperial stables were found.	Two full-scale bronze chariots found.	Ceremonial armor and helmet found, decorated with stone tiles.	Site of full-scale terracotta people discovered.	Site found with 12 terraco civil servants, and horse skeletons; another with 4(different bronze birds.

Are there subterranean rivers of mercury in the tomb of Qin Shi Huang?

Judging from geological analysis, Sima Qian's description (145–85 BCE) of the tomb of Qin Shi Huang is closer to reality than had been expected. In the area surrounding the tomb, there have been high levels of mercury detected in the ground. The presence of this mineral could be due to the existence of rivers of mercury mentioned in the writings of Sima Qian when he described the sarcophagus chamber. The mystery will remain until it is researched.

enigmas

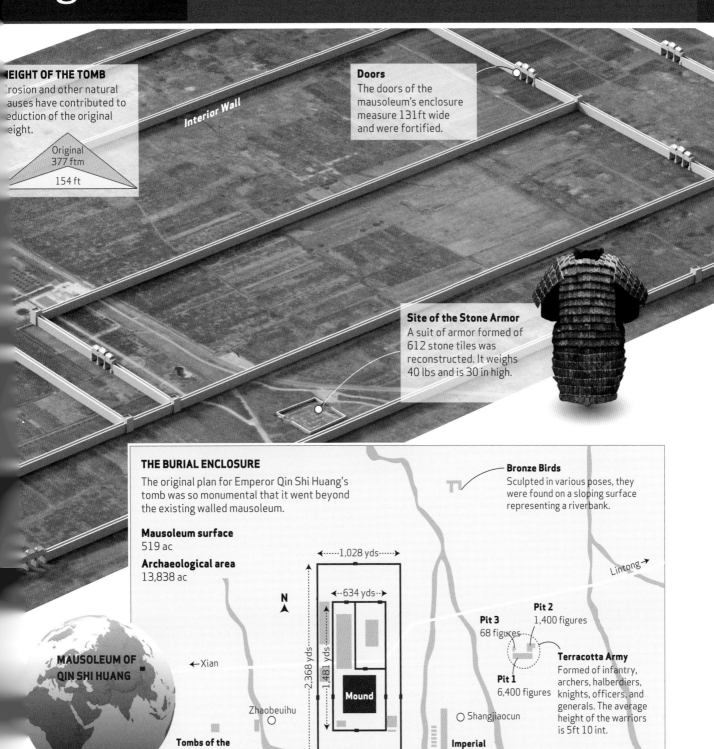

HEIGHT OF THE TOMB
Erosion and other natural causes have contributed to reduction of the original height.

Original
377 ftm
154 ft

Interior Wall

Doors
The doors of the mausoleum's enclosure measure 131ft wide and were fortified.

Site of the Stone Armor
A suit of armor formed of 612 stone tiles was reconstructed. It weighs 40 lbs and is 30 in high.

THE BURIAL ENCLOSURE
The original plan for Emperor Qin Shi Huang's tomb was so monumental that it went beyond the existing walled mausoleum.

Mausoleum surface
519 ac

Archaeological area
13,838 ac

Bronze Birds
Sculpted in various poses, they were found on a sloping surface representing a riverbank.

Lintong →

1,028 yds
634 yds
2,368 yds
1,481 yds
N

Pit 2
1,400 figures

Pit 3
68 figures

Pit 1
6,400 figures

Terracotta Army
Formed of infantry, archers, halberdiers, knights, officers, and generals. The average height of the warriors is 5ft 10 int.

← Xian

MAUSOLEUM OF QIN SHI HUANG

Zhaobeuihu

Mound

○ Shangjiaocun

Tombs of the Mausoleum Builders

Imperial Stables

The Final Resting Place

Since prehistory, the living have provided their dead with specific places and forms of final rest. These have taken the form of monuments such as mounds, more discrete forms such as columbariums, mass graves like the necropolises, and simple forms such as the anonymous grave.

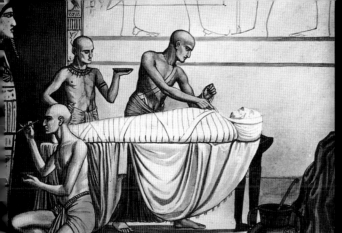

Funerary Practices

Burial is perhaps the most ancient and universal funerary practice; but cremation, ritual devouring by beasts, and releasing the body to the sea have also been widely practiced and endured. Embalming was practiced in Ancient Egypt (illustration) to preserve the body, and there has been natural mummification in dry, minimal-oxygen environments (high mountains, deserts, etc.).

ETRUSCAN TOMBS Banditaccia Necropolis, in Cerveteri (Italy), with Etruscan funerary gravestones from the third and fourth centuries BCE.

What Is the Tomb of Qin Shi Huang Hiding?

It is one of the most important archaeological sites in history. However, the majority of it has not yet been excavated. The tomb of the first emperor of China is one of the most fascinating funerary mysteries yet to be solved.

In 1974, a group of farmers began to dig near mount Li, around 19 miles east of the Chinese city Xian. They were looking for water to irrigate their fields, but they discovered something very different: at a depth of 20 ft, they uncovered colored pieces of what seemed to be large human statues made of clay. They had found the first remains of a large terracotta army that had been hidden for 2000 years, guarding the eternal dream of Qin Shi Huang. They had hit on the lost mausoleum of the first emperor and unifier of China. According to ancient chronicles, in addition to the first sections of the Great Wall of China, this ruler built an enormous tomb full of marvels–an unfinished funeral enclosure of such magnitude that it took 38 years to create.

Declared a UNESCO World Heritage Site in 1987, the mausoleum of the first emperor of China remains an unsolved mystery.

THE XIAN WARRIORS

The army of terracotta soldiers situated one mile from the foot of mount Li, where the emperor's tomb is found, has special characteristics: there are 8,000 statues around 5 ft 10 in tall, each with a distinct head and face, carrying shields and uniforms that are exquisitely detailed and correspond to their military rank. The figures include; foot soldiers in combat formation, archers, crossbowmen, and carriages drawn by four horses with coachmen and soldiers. Additionally, the weapons they carry are made of bronze, with others plated with chrome.

The statues are solid from the waist down and hollow from the waist up, and the personal details, such as their beards, ears, and head decoration were done separately. Thus far, four pits with these warriors have been discovered. The first contains a complete foot soldier regiment; the second, 1,400 statues of warriors and horses, and 64 carriages; the third appears to be a representation of a general garrison, with 68 high-ranking officials, and the supreme commander's carriage, though his statue is missing. The fourth was found empty, and it is probable that it was never used, which is one of the things that led some to conclude that the burial complex was not finished. All the statues were painted in bright colors, although their brilliance disappears quickly once exposed to oxygen. Therefore the excavation in recent years was carried out with extreme

enigmas

WHY DO THE WARRIORS' FACES VARY?

The Xian warriors were not the first to stand guard over a royal tomb. Archaeologists have uncovered statues that served the same purpose in mausoleums from the preceding Zhou dynasty. However, apart from the number of troops, Qin Shi Huang's terracotta army offers two unique qualities: the height of the statues, and their considerable array of distinctive faces. Other funerary armies, before or afterward, were always made up of figures with impersonal faces. Why this variation in the faces? Perhaps the answer is that Qin Shi Huang hoped to expend his immense power beyond his death and, as a demonstration of his enormous ability, wanted to have as faithful an image as possible of the loyal and warlike troops that had exalted him in life.

UNARMED
The terracotta soldiers carried real bronze weapons. Many were stripped of them during the civil war which erupted following the emperor's death.

Horses and Tombs

According to ancient Chinese tradition, death is the continuation of earthly life in the afterlife. For that reason, the tombs contain furniture, objects, and riches which not only were intended to make the eternal life of the deceased more pleasant, but which also demonstrated their social status. The sacrifice of horses may have been a funerary demonstration of authority since the time of the ancient Shang Dynasty. In the first emperor's tomb, this demonstration was taken to a superlative level, reflecting his absolute supremacy: the horses were buried alive, imitating the royal cavalries. Terracotta replicas were made, and the carriages were copied in bronze. To the right, the emperor's Carriage of Tranquility.

care so as to avoid losing valuable information regarding the statues, which are still underground.

The warriors were perfectly aligned in formation. The floors of the pits were tiled and their sides, corners, and ceilings were reinforced with wooden beams and mats of woven fibers with plaster incorporated.

We have described the army that was created to accompany and protect the emperor on his final journey, but what is his tomb like? What does it contain? Still awaiting excavation, the tomb has a pyramidal form and is 164 ft high. It is in a hidden location, following very specific guidelines dictated by a very ancient geomantic tradition. The burial mound complex is protected by interior and exterior walls, which surround an area of 518 ac. At the end of the 1970s various funerary buildings were discovered to the north of this wall, which probably formed part of a wing of the Dream Palace (a metaphoric allusion to death), in which a number of the emperor's concubines may have been buried. Nevertheless, almost nothing has emerged regarding the characteristics and contents of the royal tomb.

CHRONICLES OF SIMA QIAN

All that is known about the mausoleum is credited to Sima Qian, a historian who lived during the Han dynasty. His book *Shi Ji* (Historical Memories), states, among other things, that during its construction, "three underground channels were dug out for dumping copper melted in the area outside the tomb, while the burial chamber was filled with model palaces, towers, and public buildings, as well as valuable utensils, precious stones and curious objects." Thanks to the translations of Sima Qian's work, we know that by the emperor's authority, "on the outside of the chamber, the artisans placed automatic crossbows capable of killing any tomb raiders caught in the act," and that inside it "they made artificial rivers of mercury flow mechanically, imitating the Yellow and Yangtze rivers and the ocean." "On the upper part," the historian said, "they painted the firmament with all of the constellations,

Slaves and Debts

According to historical records, the 700,000 people that worked in Qin Shi Huang's mausoleum were part of three different groups. The first group being technicians and artisans who managed the operation; the second prisoners of war and enslaved individuals from all over the Empire; and the third made up of criminals and those convicted for owing debts. During this period, whoever broke the law had to pay a fine. If they could not pay it, they were sent to work. Many workers died because of the arduous work conditions. The expert artisans ended up buried alive alongside the emperor's coffin, condemned to keep the secrets of the tomb forever.

Qin Shi Huang

Considered the founder of the centralized and totalitarian Chinese Empire which lasted for millennia, Qin Shi Huang (259–210 BCE) is a legendary ruler, akin to Alexander the Great or Julius Cesar in the West. He unified the country, the language, the currency, the units of measurement, and the length of the shafts of Chinese carriages. He created a bureaucratic system based on merit and began the work on the Great Wall of China. An audacious and cruel strategist, he conquered rival kingdoms in merely a decade. One of his great obsessions was the quest for immortality.

while the Earth was represented on the lower part." Other translators describe the ceiling of the room as, "bronze, sprinkled with gems, as if it was a star-strewn sky." In any case, none of this has been seen by anyone alive today. The great mausoleum of Qin Shi Huang still retains its mystery, as well as the corpses of all those whom destiny made "assistants of the eternal dream" of the emperor who made China one single kingdom. We don't know how many "assistants" there were, but we have a good idea of how they died. Sima Qian said: "Immediately after the emperor was placed in the burial chamber, surrounded by his treasures, the interior and exterior doors were closed, imprisoning all those who had worked in his mausoleum. Nobody could get out." According to the historical narrative, the barren concubines who had not had children with the emperor were also buried alive in their emperor's mausoleum. When technology is available to permit extensive exploration, these dark secrets will be unveiled.

Archaeological Excavation

Excavating a tomb is an enormous undertaking, requiring coordination between numerous professionals. This is all the more true when the site is as colossal as the one at Xian, which presents technical difficulties as well. For these reasons, the majority of this burial enclosure has yet to be excavated.

Where to Start

Before commencing an excavation, preliminary data must be gathered concerning the site by surveying the surface and performing archaeological tests. Other preparations must also be carried out: requesting permits, formulating a proposal, and evaluating what tools are needed. After all that, the most appropriate method and procedures for the excavation are decided upon.

10,000 ARTIFACTS
The Xian archaeological team has already unearthed over 10,000 artifacts.

TOOLS
In an excavation, brushes, brooms, picks, shovels, wheelbarrows, buckets, rakes, measuring instruments, and cameras are used, among other tools.

1 PREPARING THE GROUND

Before excavation, it is best to clear the surface of the ground to eliminate vegetation and any debris present. Then a sounding is taken to study the strata of the terrain and divide up the terrain according to the selected work method. Measuring lines are placed to mark the exact location of the artifacts.

2 EXCAVATE AND RECORD ACTIONS TAKEN

The terrain is now ready to be excavated. Earth is extracted until the first artifacts are found. It is essential to keep exhaustive records of the actions taken, making thorough notes on the data collected for each discovery.

3 CLEANING THE ARTIFACTS

As walls, pieces of art, or any other type of artifact are found, they are carefully cleaned using different kinds of brushes. If necessary, the objects are sprayed with water so the dirt gives way more easily. Cleaning is sometimes done outside the site.

The Xian Dilemma

Unfortunately, the majority of the vivid original colors of the terracotta warriors have been lost due to oxidation. This happened just five hours after they were unearthed. For this reason, some archaeologists believe that more advanced technology is needed before proceeding with the excavation of the Qin Shi Huang mausoleum, while others think that this should not be a deterrent.

THOUSANDS OF PIECES

The nearly 8,000 warriors were made in pieces. The torso and appendages were made with molds, while the faces were personalized: no two are alike. Reconstructing the figures was a real puzzle for the archaeologists.

YELLOW EARTH

To mold the figures, "yellow earth" was used, which is present in the area surrounding the mausoleum.

REPRODUCING THE PROCESS

To understand exactly how the figures were created, the archaeologists of Xian had to recreate the entire process. The shaping, baking, and finishing of the warriors were tested using various methods until they matched the technique employed by the artisans according to Emperor Qin Shi Huang's orders.

6 RESTORATION AND CONCLUSIONS

Along with the restoration of damaged artifacts—in Xian, many figures had to be reconstructed, as shown in the photo—the team of archaeologists begins analyzing the results of the excavation. Conclusions are published afterwards in the form of a memorandum, report, or article.

4 PROTECTING THE ARTIFACTS

In many cases, the discovered artifacts demand special protection to keep them from deteriorating upon contact with oxygen. In the case of the terracotta warriors, it was necessary, as shown in the image, to spray the figures with chemicals to prevent deterioration.

5 CLASSIFICATION

Once the work of excavating the tomb is complete, the artifacts need to be classified. A serial number is given to each artifact—a procedure known as cataloging—and an informational inventory is created.

What Happened to the Bog Bodies?

Since the nineteenth century, more than a thousand mummified bodies have appeared in the peat bogs of northern Europe. The majority of them have one distinctive feature in common: they died violently.

They are known as the "bog bodies" because they appeared after being submerged in the peat bogs of northern Europe–namely Germany, Denmark, the UK, and Ireland–for around 2,000 years. The lack of oxygen in these wetlands inhibits the natural decay of organic material, which is why bodies have been dicovered dating back to the middle of the Iron Age, 2,500 years ago. While they were discovered in different places, they have common characteristics: almost all the bodies had a violent death. Nearly all of them show marks or the remains of rope around the neck area, with evident signs of having been hit, but without traces of blood. Many were decapitated or stabbed, while others were thrown into the bog when they were still alive and drowned. Almost all were naked and had a birch rod on or stuck into their body. Were they sacrificed to the gods? Were they condemned people, executed according to some specific ritual? Were they prisoners or criminals sentenced to death?

RITUAL SACRIFICE

The experts are arriving at a number of conclusions. It is already known that in northern Europe the bogs were considered sacred to the majority of the people that lived there. Deities such as Nerthus–the goddess of the earth honored by the inhabitants of the Jutland peninsula–reside there, and the bog bodies could have been sacrificed to her; and some link their deaths with fertility rituals. The Roman historians Pliny and Tacitus recorded that these people had the custom of drowning criminals, deserters, traitors, and adulterers in bogs. Julius Cesar noted that peat bog sacrifices were common practice after winning a battle, and that they were done in honor of the gods of war. Analysis of the contents of the victims' stomachs seems to confirm the ritual sacrifice theory, because they have shown the consumption of certain products known to have been consumed in the religious ceremonies of that period. This was the case with the bog body named the "Lindow Man," discovered near Manchester in 1984. He was found with mistletoe fruit in his stomach, which leads to the conjecture that he was the victim of a Celtic ritual. In the stomach of the Grauballe Man were remains of rye ergot, which indicates that he may have been drugged.

The Tollund Man

The Tollund Man was discovered in a bog in Denmark in 1950, and is the most well-known of the thousand-plus bodies that have appeared in the northern European peat bogs. This Scandinavian tribe member from the fourth century BCE is 5 ft. 2 in. tall (1.6 m) and was 30 or 40 years old when he died. Dressed in only a leather cap and a belt, the rope around his neck, which he was strangled with, was preserved. One difference between the Tollund Man and others showing evident signs of cruelty is the calm expression on his face, suggesting that he has accepted his fate as a victim of ritual sacrifice with resignation, and that someone took pity on him and deposited his body in the waters of the bog.

Who Was Ötzi the Iceman?

The Iceman has been named Ötzi and is the oldest mummy in Europe. He was discovered in 1991 in an alpine glacier, and tools were found next to the body which have taught us a lot about life 5,300 years ago.

On September-ber 19, 1991, a pair of German hikers, Helmut and Erika Simon, were alarmed to discover a human body protruding from a half-frozen puddle in the Alpine valley of Ötzi, between Italy and Austria. They believed there had been an accident and told the police, who immediately pulled the body out. Surprisingly, it was the body of a man who had died 5,300 years earlier. He was mummified and very well preserved. A 6 ft. 1 in. (1.85 m) bow made of yew wood was found beside him, as well as material for building 14 viburnum wood arrows, and two finished arrows with guide feathers and flint arrowheads attached to the wood with birch sap and string. Also alongside him were a birch bark bag, a raffia fiber rope, a flint knife with an ash wood handle, a chisel, a bear skin cloak, a little tinder and pyrite for making fire, a deer hide band, and a copper hatchet with a lime tree wood handle. He had a wound on his hand and an arrowhead had entered through his back and punctured his left lung. How did he die? DNA analysis revealed the blood of other people on the cloak and knife, as well as two different blood types on the arrow he carried. He probably died of blood loss after a battle with rivals.

BIOLOGICAL ANALYSIS

Ötzi was studied in depth. He was 5 ft. 5 in. (1.65 m) tall, was not over 45 years old, and must have weighed 110 lbs.(49.9 kg) The pollen found on his body was analyzed and revealed information regarding wheat and legume crops in his surroundings. The remains of his digestive system led to the conclusion that he had eaten twice recently: a meal of chamois meat and another of deer meat, and that he had consumed cereals, sloe, and some roots.

The presence of parallel lines tattooed on his left wrist, lumbar area, and both legs, coinciding with signs of arthritis, led to the conclusion that they had some magic-curative purpose. His clothing was quite sophisticated. He wore a leather vest and cloak. His footwear was water resistant and designed for use in snow, although it could have been the upper part of some kind of snow shoe.

Ötzi the Iceman was an extremely intelligent man from the Copper Age–an artisan, hunter, and perhaps also shepherd and farmer, capable of living 10,500 ft. (267 m) above sea level.

STONE DISC AMULET

ARROWS AND QUIVER

Ötzi's Tools

Several primitive tools that appear to have belonged to him were found alongside the mummy. With the exception of a kind of amulet, the majority were used for survival in a hostile environment: bow and arrows, flint knife, copper ax and fire-making tools. This material has been very useful to archaeologists, who have been able to determine the degree of sophistication of the Iceman, as demonstrated by the plant fiber sheath for the knife and the ax with its handle and fastenings, which are the first intact examples of their kind.

HORN AND STONE CHISELS

COPPER AX

FLINT KNIFE AND FIBER SHEATH

PRESERVATION
The well-preserved state in which Ötzi was found revealed that he suffered from Lyme disease, cavities, and cardio-vascular problems.

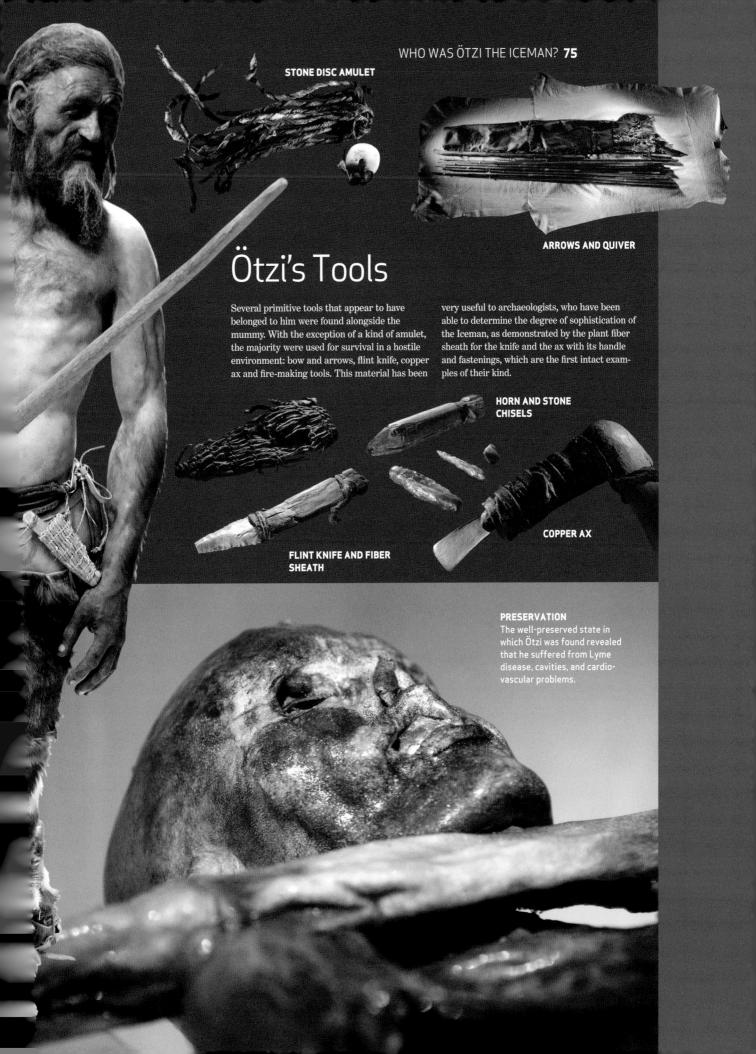

What Mysteries Surround the Lord of Sipán?

In 1987, one of the most impressive tombs in the Americas was found in northern Peru: that of the Lord of Sipán. Jewels beyond compare were found inside, along with several other cadavers, including a dog and two llamas.

His body rests in an enormous burial complex in the Lambayeque Valley, 17.5 miles (28 km) from the city of Chiclayo. The site covers almost 74 acres (30 ha) and includes three grand components: two monumental structures, which would have been used for holding religious ceremonies, and a large funerary mound made of adobe, begun in the second century and used for 500 years. This archaeological complex, which was given the name of Huaca Rajada and is considered one of the most important sites in the history of the Americas, was built by the Moche people, a rich culture that arose on the northern coast of Peru, a thousand years before the Inca, and flourished between the first and seventh centuries. It was a culture of artists, farmers, fishermen, and warriors, which reached a high level of development and had a complex social organization. The Moche were pottery and metalworking experts, and also great architects. They built enormous adobe buildings, truncated pyramids that were accessed via ramps and decorated with yellow and red paint, and polychromatic reliefs featuring representations of their gods.

OFFERINGS AND SACRIFICES

They believed in life after death, which persons of superior rank would enter taking a wealth of offerings, including jewels and ceremonial objects made of gold and silver, objects of copper, turquoise, and lapis lazuli, spondylus shells (which are large, red-orange and purple, very striking and with unusual spines), ceramic vases, ornaments, and various types of weapons and insignia denoting power. They are also accompanied by other persons and animals into this new life. Inside his tomb, alongside the Lord of Sipán, a powerful Moche ruler from the third century, eight other people were buried: two young women and one older woman, a child, a military general, a standard-bearer, a watchman, and a guardian who was missing both legs. All these people accompanied their ruler on his final journey, and it is very probable that, believing that they would continue serving him in another life, they gracefully accepted their deaths in a ritual sacrifice. Along with them, two llamas and a dog were also sacrificed.

This tomb, though the most well-known, is not the only tomb in the large Moche complex. In the burial mound of Sipán, which means "House of the Moon," or

enigmas

DID WOMEN SIT ON THE MOCHE THRONES?

The discovery in 2006 of a mummy from the fourth century in the Huaca Cao Viejo pertaining to a woman of high rank, wearing insignia denoting power, has led archaeologists to believe that a feminine dynasty of queen-priests existed in the first centuries of the Moche culture in the Chicama Valley. Until the discovery of the mummy, now known as the Señora de Cao, it had been thought that the Moche society was, politically, essentially patriarchal.

SEÑORA DE CAO
Recreation of the Señora de Cao, a powerful Moche ruler who died when she was between 30 and 40 years old.

REEVALUATION
The discovery of the Lord of Sipán's tomb meant reevaluating of what was known of the Moche culture, placing them among the peoples who made up Andean civilization.

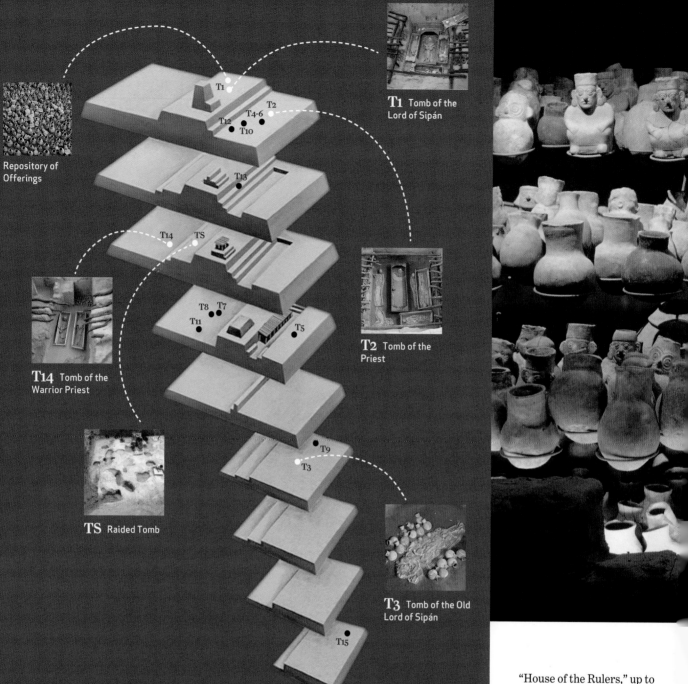

Repository of Offerings

T1 Tomb of the Lord of Sipán

T1

T2

T12   T4-6
    T10

T13

T14   TS

T14 Tomb of the Warrior Priest

T2 Tomb of the Priest

T8   T7
T11
        T5

TS Raided Tomb

T9
T3

T3 Tomb of the Old Lord of Sipán

T15

Layers of Tombs

Huaca Rajada is an ancient site that is both ceremonial and sacred. The Moche burial site originally consisted of a stepped pyramid of adobe, but many centuries after its construction, it has been excavated by so many grave robbers that it is now divided into two mounds united by the remains of its central section. This gives rise to its name: Huaca Rajada, the Torn Grave.

Phenomena such as the torrential rains of "El Niño" have also contributed to its deterioration. Traditionally, the upper platform was reserved for ceremonial functions. The lower sections housed the mausoleum, where high-level dignitaries of Moche society were buried. However, Huaca Rajada corresponds to an era during which ceremonial and funerary functions were juxta-

posed in these sacred sites. As the pyramid was restructured for reasons of maintenance or prestige, new levels were added and new platforms were built on top. Eight architectural construction phases have been detected. The tomb of the Lord of Sipán is found on the top level, while that of the "Old Lord of Sipán" is in one of the lowest levels.

"House of the Rulers," up to eight different construction phases corresponding to different eras and hierarchies have been identified. Between 1987 and 2000, six construction phases were discovered, in which as many as thirteen different burial sites were excavated. Between 2007 and 2009 two more phases were found, with two new Moche tombs and up to fifty tombs corresponding to later cultures, such as the Lambayeque, Chimú, and Chimú-Inca. Among those of the Moche

Repository of Offerings

Before discovering the Lord of Sipán's tomb, archaeologists found a repository of offerings–a chamber replete with ceramic objects. According to the description of the excavators, in this room they found, in addition to 1,137 ceramic pieces: four copper crowns, a mask, shells, various minor objects, human remains, and dozens of llama bones. Of the ceramics discovered, those with anthropomorphous features belonging to the classic epoch were predominant. The Moche culture is known for its ceramics, which until the discovery of the tombs had been the primary source of information for archaeologists and anthropologists about this culture. Their sculptural finesse that evolved over time masterfully combined utility and art. They created sculptures that realistically reproduced natural scenes, animals, divinities, economic and sexual activities, portraits, etc., documenting them for all time. Ceramic materials were also placed in the tomb of the Moche ruler, displayed in an orderly fashion and with ritual finality.

culture, each has a different burial format, and that belonging to "the Priest," a contemporary of the Lord of Sipán, has special importance. This body wore a headdress of owl feathers, held a copper cup in his right hand, and was flanked by the bodies of two young women, a guardian missing his feet, another young man, a child, a dog, a snake, and a headless llama.

Also notable are the tombs of the "Warrior Priest" and, above all, that of the "Old Lord of Sipán," dated some 100 years earlier (three or four generations at that time), in which only the remains of two "companions" were found: a woman and a llama. The offerings accompanying him, more complex and varied than those of the Lord of Sipán, lead archaeologists to believe he may have been a warrior-priest, a ruler who fulfilled both political and religious functions.

TREASURE AND LOOTERS
Huaca Rajada, where a magnificent museum opened in 2009 to display many of the marvels found there, continues to be excavated, safe from the grave robbers who, in the eighties, almost managed to make off with its magnificent riches.

When archaeologists led by Peruvian Walter Alva began to work at the site, more than a hundred large holes and tons of debris made the intentions of the treasure seekers clear. They had already stripped several tombs of their treasures, though it is not known whether any of them struck it rich by robbing the tombs of the old lords of Sipán. However, more than one of them became ill. Their ailments have been attributed to the practice of spreading cinnabar dust–a substance that releases toxic gases upon contact with air–in the tombs of Moche aristocrats before sealing them, for the purpose of discouraging tomb raiders. In this way, the priests attempted to ensure that no one disturbed the journey to the Other Side of those who, from their new lives, would continue looking out for their people.

The Royal Treasures of Sipán

The Museum of the Royal Tombs of Sipán in Peru contains many objects found among the funerary offerings surrounding the high-level Moche dignitaries buried in Huaca Rajada. The tombs housed a great diversity of offerings, the most exquisite being those of the Lord of Sipán and the Old Lord of Sipán.

The Tumbaga Method

The Moche were extraordinarily distinguished goldsmiths, displaying mastery in the smelting of precious metals. They not only smelted copper, gold, and silver, but also laminated, shaped, embossed, and soldered them. In their metalwork, they developed complex techniques to give the appearance of gold to objects that were in reality copper, impressing experts to this day. To do this, they used a method called "tumbaga," which was widely used among pre-Columbian societies in Central and South America. This technique consists of a process of depletion gilding, generally with an alloy of 90% copper and 10% gold. The metal mixure was submerged in ammonia baths to oxidize the copper.

Following this, the alloy was hammered to bring the gold to the surface, while the copper remained in the interior of the sheet.

NECKLACE BEADS
Beads in the shape of an old man's head. While these particular beads of gold belong to the funerary offerings of the Old Lord of Sipán, necklaces with similarly shaped beads made of gold and silver often formed part of the funerary offerings for Moche aristocrats.

NARIGUERA
Spectacular ceremonial nariguera (nose-ring) of the Old Lord of Sipán. Made of gold and silver, it shows the form of a dignitary with his weapons wearing a headdress featuring a bat.

CRAB GOD BREASTPLATE
As a society of fishermen, the Moche modeled their gods after the marine life surrounding them. This ornament in the shape of a crab, belonging to the Old Lord of Sipán, is an example.

CEREMONIAL DIADEM
Unique diadem with a double representation. The first, impersonal, displays an anatomical discrepancy in simultaneously showing the back and palm of the hand. The central figure, the God of Ulluchu, repeats the gesture.

DEITY OF THE ULLUCHU
Gilded copper adornment representing the God of Ulluchu; ulluchu are seeds with anticoagulant properties appearing in blood offerings to Aia Paec, "the Decapitator," the supreme god of the Moche pantheon

Royal Scepter

The scepter of the Lord of Sipán, a symbol of his supreme power, displays the insignias of power denoting the Moche sovereign. The reliefs carved on the inverted pyramid represent the Lord with his warrior garb and combat mace imposing his will on the enemy, a common image on the scepters found. Elements of military equipment are recreated on the scepter's handle. Combat maces and slingshots can be distinguished on its sides. The silver blade would have been used in the ritual sacrifice of prisoners.

BREASTPLATE
Radial breastplate made of different colored Spondylus shells. Based on solar symbolism, it alludes to the Lord as the maintainer of social and religious order.

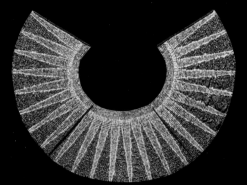

FELINE HEAD
Feline representation of the supreme god with jaws set with shell incrustations.

COXALERA
Gold adornment that hung from the waist with a fold at the top that held a rattle. It is made in the shape of the ceremonial knife of the supreme god Aia Paec.

GOLD PEANUTS
Peanut shells that formed part of a necklace for the Lord of Sipán, in total consisting of ten gold shells and ten silver.

UCKLE AND RATTLE
old embossed openwork buckle with he image of the god Aia Paec. The rbs contain copper grains that, when haken, convert it into a rattle. The uckle was fastened to a belt.

GOLD MASK
Stylized gold mask with the face of a Moche man, discovered in the tomb of the Lord of Sipán.

FELINE DIVINITY
Unique anthropomorphic figure of Aia Paec, represented as a feline divinity with an owl-headed serpent headdress. Found in the funerary offerings of the Old Lord of Sipán. The figure formed part of a headdress.

BREASTPLATE AND MASK
Octopus breastplate based on ritual representations of Aia Paec—the principal Moche divinity—belonging to the Old Lord of Sipán, and funerary mask with nariguera found in the same tomb.

Why Are There Celtic Mummies in China?

In 2000 BCE a group of men, women, and children were buried in Asia. Their mummies were found in 1934. Their features, red and blonde hair and light-colored eyes, betrayed their Celtic origins. What were they doing there?

In the so-called "Small River Cemetery," discovered by Swedish archaeologist Folke Bergman in Lop Nur in the Chinese region of Xinjiang in 1934, more than 30 very special mummies were found. Not much attention was paid to them until almost 70 years later. Only in 2003 did scientists begin to study their features and conclude that they are Indo-European, as their red and blonde hair and light-colored eyes indicate. The sands of the salt desert of Taklamakan preserved the bodies practically intact. The oldest is dated at 3,980 years. DNA analysts, furthermore, corroborated scientific suspicions: they belonged to an unknown Paleo-European culture originating in the Bronze Age. What were they doing in the middle of what would later become the Silk Road, in an area where the Chinese arrived for the first time in 300 BCE?

FUNERARY COMPLEX
The discovery forms part of the large Xiaohe funerary complex, which contains some 350 tombs, although archaeological explorations done between 1970 and 2010 in the Tarim River basin have brought to light more than 500 interments and hundreds of mummies that raise many more questions than answers. The most spectacular–better preserved than the Egyptian mummies–were in a type of coffin shaped like an upside-down boat hull covered with ox hides, and were dressed in very sophisticated fabrics (some with designs similar to those of the tartans of the Scottish clans) and surrounded by offerings in beautifully decorated baskets. Unusual masks of wood and metal have also been found. The graves are marked with posts that are almost 13 feet (4 m) tall, some of which are oar-shaped.

Many of the mummies, in addition to brightly colored fine fabric clothing, wore felt hats with feathers (similar to Tyrolean headdresses) and pointed caps. Others had two blue stones over their eyes, such as one young child wrapped in brown fabric with a blue and red cord circling it five times.

Their blonde hair, light-colored eyes, straight noses, larger stature (some of the women reached 6 ft 3 in, or 1.9 m), and clothing are Celtic features. Analysis has corroborated their origin, which has manifested an unexpected connection between Europe and Asia that questions the accepted theories about relationships between human communities before written history.

enigmas

WERE THERE ALSO CAUCASIAN POPULATIONS IN THE FAR EAST?

At the end of the nineteenth century, the Ainu, the indigenous people of the Hokkaido and Kuril Islands in the north of Japan and the Russian island of Sakhalin, presented a challenge to anthropologists. Their facial features and complexion–below is a photo of an Ainu man taken in 1904– were more Caucasian than Asian. Their existence led to the understanding that they were descendants of a Paleo-Siberian population from the taiga that reached the Japanese islands in the Paleolithic period, and that they shared many European features, as affirmed by British anthropologist Arnold Henry Savage Landor and Japanese linguist Kyosuke Kindaichi. However, after centuries of genetic evolution, recent DNA analysis has shown that the Ainu no longer are linked to genetic groups of European origin.

SUBESHI
Witches of Subeshi,"
om the fourth cen-
n Turin and named
nted hats.

SALT DESERT
The climate of the Taklamakan Desert has helped to preserve the more than 300 Caucasian mummies found in the burial complex at Xiahoe, in the Chinese region of Xinjiang.

Who Was the Real Discoverer of Sipán?

According to some of those living near the Huaca Rajada archaeological complex in

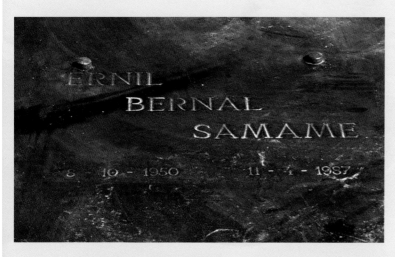

TOMB OF ERNIL BERNAL SAMAMÉ
Burial place of the Peruvian "huaquero" who some consider the rightful discoverer of the tombs of Sipán.

the Lambayeque Valley in Peru, the authentic discoverer of the tomb of the Lord of Sipán was not the well-known Peruvian archaeologist Walter Alva, but a young "huaquero" (grave robber) named Ernil Bernal Samamé, who, because of his criminal background, was denied credit for the discovery. It is considered by many that disinterring a body, even hundreds or thousands of years

after it was buried, brings the risk of being "punished" by the ghost of the deceased, especially if that person was important and was carrying treasures on their journey to the other side. This seems to have happened to Ernil, originally from the Sipán area, who was killed under unusual circumstances in 1987, the

same year the famous tomb was discovered. It has never been discovered why or by whom the "huaquero" was gunned down, although it has been pointed out that his death occurred during a police operation in the area, after they had been made aware that Huaca Rajada was being looted and had subsequently established a presence in the area to end this practice.

Could "Ötzi's Curse" Exist?

In April of 2005, the Austrian archaeologist Konrad Spindler died in Innsbruck, Austria, at 66 years of age. The archaeologist had examined the Ice Man in depth and had, with his groundbreaking work, contributed to making the 5,300 year-old mummy of the snow hunter famous worldwide. His death could have gone unnoticed by the masses, but it had certain repercussions: he was the fifth person related to the mummy of the Ice Man to die, which made some think that there truly was a curse. The first to lose their life was the doctor Rainer Kenn, the forensic examiner who analyzed the mummy immediately after it was found, who died in a traffic accident in 1992. His death was followed by that of a mountaineer who guided the climber Reinhold Meisssner to the location of the find and was subsequently buried in an avalanche. Shortly thereafter, a reporter who filmed a documentary about Ötzi also died. And, after that, Helmut Simon, the mummy's discoverer, was found dead in the Alps in 2004. Konrad Spinder is the last … for the moment.

Was Qin Shi Huang Assassinated?

The tomb of the first emperor of China, Qin Shi Huang, was conceived as a monument to immortality. In life, the emperor was obsessed with death and researched all possible ways to defeat it. In fact, he traveled tirelessly throughout China in search of the elixir of eternal youth, and died on one of those journeys, in Eastern China, on an expedition that sought to find the legendary islands of the immortals and to come away with the secret of eternal life. Qin Shi Huang wanted to "last as long as the earth and sky, move through the water without getting wet, and walk through fire without getting burned." It is clear that he did not manage to live forever, although the secrets held by his tomb, which was designed to be an authentic cosmic diagram, still have not been revealed. Everything indicates that Qin Shi Huang died at 49 years of age upon ingesting mercury, the basic ingredient for a supposed elixir that would have granted him immortality. But, while some consider that the poison was consumed in his search for eternal life, others insist that the emperor was poisoned. In reality, little is known of the circumstances surrounding his death.

Why Were the Bog Bodies Pierced with a Stake?

The fact that the majority of the bog mummies of Northern Europe were found with a large birch stake piercing the body has been interpreted by some researchers as a magic ritual. This practice would have been intended to prevent the bodies of those thrown into the bogs from returning from the world of the dead to seek vengeance and torment those who, in life, were their executioners. This custom has also been related to the practice, very common in some Eastern European countries many centuries before, of driving a stake through the heart of particular persons when it was believed that they might return from the dead, as vampires, to drink the blood of the living.

QIN SHI HUANG
Portrait of the first unifier of China, who governed the empire from 221 to 210 BCE.

Are the Mummies of Tarim Tocharians?

In opposition to theories defending the Celtic origins of the Tarim mummies, some specialists believe that these mummies belong to the Tocharian people, an ancient alliance of Caucasian tribes speaking the Indo-European language that dominated Central Asia, who were related to the Scythians and the Kurgan cultures. The Hindus called them Kushan, and Chinese chronicles refer to them as the Yuezhi. Some tribes from this culture settled to the north of the Great Wall, in the Chinese province now known as Inner Mongolia. They were driven out in the second century BCE by the Xiongnu nomads, and took refuge in the Sogdiana and Bactriana regions in Afghanistan, from where they launched the conquest of India in the second century CE. In contrast with the older Tarim mummies, the tall, blonde Yingpan Man (third and fourth centuries CE) would not have been a native of the area, but a Sogdian trader, a descendent of the Tocharians, who died far from home in a station of some importance along the Silk Road.

THE YINGPAN MAN
One of the mummies found in Xinjiang. It was entombed with a mask.

Did They Worship Mummies in the Americas?

Chilean anthropologist Bernardo T. Arriaza, author of the book *Beyond Death: The Chinchorro Mummies of Ancient Chile*, states that the Chinchorro people did not fear the dead. To them, their mummies were "living bodies" that housed the souls of the dead. They considered them a link between the world of the living and the other side, and were convinced that the mummies, imbued with ancestral knowledge and the wisdom of past generations, were valid interlocutors that cooperated with the living. Subsequently, the mummies participated in the community's religious and social festivals and were present for all important acts.

This devotion is the oldest demonstration of mummy worship recorded among the South American peoples. Certain later pre-Inca cultures also worshipped mummies, which they carried in processions. Considered symbols of community unity, their destruction was a priority for enemy peoples.

Did the Inuit Bury Their Dead Relatives?

Until the last century, it was believed that, because of the inhospitable climatic conditions, the Inuit or Eskimos who lived in Greenland did not bury their dead. Instead, it was thought that their bodies were abandoned and later devoured by wild animals. However, in 1972, eight bodies mummified by the cold were discovered in very good condition in a cave near the abandoned Inuit settlement of Qilakitsoq, on the western coast of Greenland. The bodies were those of a six-month-old baby, a four-year-old child, and six women ranging from 18 to 50 years of age who had died five centuries before.

Did the Moche Offer Sacrifices to End Droughts?

Archaeology has revealed over the years that the upper castes of the Moche society offered human sacrifices to their bloodthirsty god Aia Paec, which when translated means "the Decapitator," or "the Executioner." Commonly, this involved prisoners of war who were subjected to a complex ritual, reserved for priests and Moche aristocracy. After being forced to fight one another to the death, the surviving prisoners were sacrificed to the supreme Moche deity. Prior to the sacrifice, the victims were administered ulluchu, a fruit with anticoagulant properties, and a psychotropic substance. Afterward, the victim's throat was slit, and their blood was collected in a cup and then drunk by the high priest or by the Moche ruler before being offered to Aia Paec and very likely sprinkled over their crops. Some aracheologists believe that the victims' flesh was also removed from their bodies, and that their skeletons were then covered in clay. It seems that the Moche civilization, located in an arid region of the Peruvian coast, offered human sacrifices to their supreme god to seek the blessing of rain in times of drought.

PRISONER
Relief showing a line of Moche prisoners in Huaca Cao Viejo.

To See and Visit

▼ **OTHER PLACES OF INTEREST**

MUSEUM OF THE ROYAL TOMBS OF SIPÁN
SIPÁN, PERU

As the visitor descends into the heart of the museum, they find the Royal Moche Room, in which the Lord of Sipán, the main attraction in this collection, rests. In addition to mummies, the museum has a valuable collection of gold artifacts, clothing, jewels, and the various objects making up the funerary offerings of the Moche culture.

SOUTH TYROL MUSEUM OF ARCHAEOLOGY
BOLZANO, ITALY

The Ötzi mummy, "the Iceman," is displayed in this museum in a chamber emulating the glacial conditions that kept him exceptionally well-preserved for more than 3,000 years. In addition to the original items found with

Ötzi (tools and ropes), the museum has replicas that recreate life in the Alps during the Bronze Age.

NATIONAL MUSEUM OF IRELAND
DUBLIN, IRELAND

In 2003, this museum established a research program to find out more about the bog bodies found in various areas throughout the country. The show "Kingship and Sacrifice" offered a new theory that connects human sacrifice to rites of power in the Iron Age; specifically, it is believed that human sacrifices, and the depositing of bodies in the bogs, only took place with the arrival of a new king or sovereign. The results of this research show not only the findings made in Ireland, but also findings that relate to a

XIAN, CHINA

WARRIORS

The enormous Museum of Qin Terracotta Warriors and Horses lies 19 mi from the city of Xian. Covering more than 170,000 square feet (15,795 sq m), it displays all of the figures excavated from these underground tombs since 1979. After more than three decades of work, around 7,000 figures—cera-mics, soldiers, carriages, horses, and weapons—have been unearthed. Almost all have been restored.

HISTORY MUSEUM

Ancient Chinese civilization was born in the province of Shaanxi, and the city of Xian was its capital for more than 1,000 years. Thirteen different imperial dynasties were established and reigned here. This museum, built in 1983, hou-ses an impressive collection of items that present the country's history through various pieces and exhibits. The exhibit portraying the invention of paper merits special attention.

TOMB

The emperor's tomb is just a few miles from the museum. It has been cal-culated that building the entire funerary complex, which covers nearly 15,000 acres (6,070 ha), took 38 years. In addition to the terracotta army, the com-plex includes around 400 tombs. The emperor's tomb is found under a hill, which is essentially a gravestone standing 375 feet (114 m) tall, and has not yet been excavated.

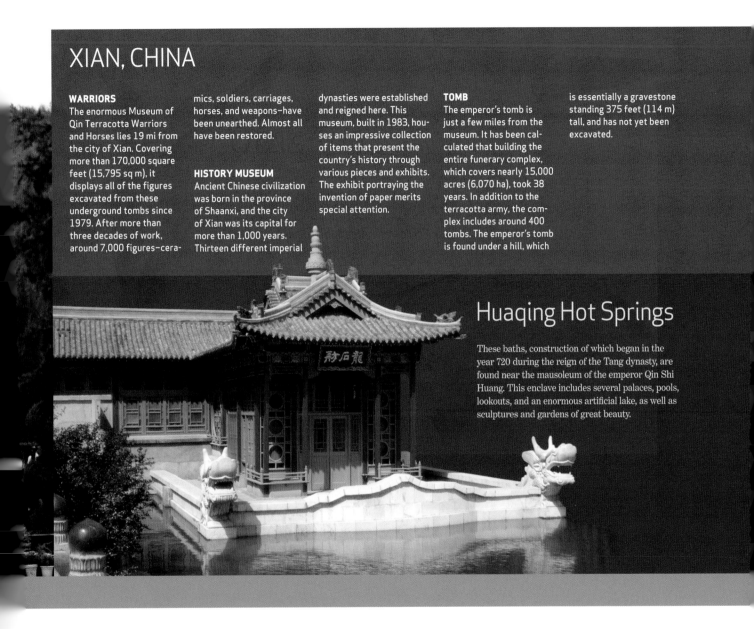

Huaqing Hot Springs

These baths, construction of which began in the year 720 during the reign of the Tang dynasty, are found near the mausoleum of the emperor Qin Shi Huang. This enclave includes several palaces, pools, lookouts, and an enormous artificial lake, as well as sculptures and gardens of great beauty.

broader European context involving countries such as the United Kingdom, Denmark, the Netherlands and Germany, where similar dis-coveries have been made.

SILKEBORG MUSEUM
SILKEBORG, DENMARK

The Tollund Man, one of the best known "Bog Bodies" in the world, is found at this museum in central Denmark. The Elling Woman, another mummy from the area, is also on dis-play here. She was found before the Tollund Man, and it is presumed that she was sacri-ficed in some kind of ritual. The museum has created an exhibition on the early Iron Age, in which replicas of clothing from that era, smelting ovens, tools, and other objects are highlighted.

DRENTS MUSEUM
ASSEN, NETHERLANDS

This museum in the Dutch city of Assen, to the south of Gronigen, houses one of the most important collections of bog mummies in all of Europe. Within the collection, the Yde Girl, the Weerdinge Men, the Exloërmond Man, and Emmer-Erscheidenveen Man stand out. Other striking pieces include the oldest canoe in the world, made between 8200 and 7600 BCE, and various metal funerary objects. This museum also has a rich collection of objects from the Funnelbeaker culture which fused Neolithic and Mesolithic techniques in Central Europe.

Glossary

BOG BODIES Mummified bodies that have appeared in the peat bogs of northern Europe, all of which appeared to have experienced violent deaths.

BRONZE AGE A period of ancient civilization that was characterized by the use of bronze, beginning between 4000 and 3000 BCE, before the Iron Age.

CURSE OF TUTANKHAMEN A situation in which it was believed that those who attended the unveiling of Tutankhamen's tomb, or had violated it or touched it in some interpretations, were dying due to the deceased pharaoh's revenge. The deaths associated were later revealed to be coincidental.

EMBALMING The process of preserving remains of the human body through alteration to slow the decomposing process, most often for funerals and burials.

EXCAVATING Meaning to excavate, in which a person digs or tunnels to uncover something buried in the ground.

FIRMAMENT From the Bible, referring to the curve of the sky as a dome above Earth. In royal or extravagant tombs, this would refer to the ceiling, such as Qin Shi Huang's tomb in which constellations were painted on the ceiling.

FUNERARY A term describing anything involving the process of funerals or any commemoration of the dead.

GOLDEN RATIO A ratio in mathematics where two quantities' ratio is the same as that of their sum to the larger of the two quantities, equal to 1.61803398875

HAN DYNASTY China's second dynasty following the Qin Dynasty.

HERODIUM Also known as the tomb of Herod 1, or, Herod the Great, according to the first-century historian Josephus.

MAUSOLEUM A type of tomb, typically in which the dead are usually buried above ground, with their coffin inside a large stone structure.

NECROPOLIS Any exceptionally large, intricate cemetery in ancient cities.

ÖTZI THE ICEMAN A nickname given to a preserved human body found by German hikers in the Alpine Valley of Ötzi, who died 5,300 years before being uncovered.

PHYSIOGNOMY A process by which those studying the remains of a human body attempt to determine other qualities of character, mind, lifestyle, and other inner qualities believed to be signified by external appearance.

QIN SHI HUANG Known as the first emperor of a unified China, Qin Shi Huang founded the Qin Dynasty, and is commonly associated with the famous terracotta warriors in his tomb.

SARCOPHAGUS A coffin, typically of stone, used in the ancient civilizations of Egypt, Rome, and Greece, and often accompanied by statues and engravings.

SHI JI A book written about the tomb of Qin Shi Huang by the historian Sima Qian, who lived during Han Dynasty. The name translates to "Historical Memories."

TOLLUND MAN A body discovered in Denmark in 1950 among the bog bodies of northern Europe, said to be a Scandanavian tribe member from the fourth century BCE who was strangled to death and buried with the rope.

URAEUS A symbol in Ancient Egypt of an upright cobra, signifying royalty.

VISCERA The plural of viscus, which is an internal organ of the human body typically in the chest or upper cavity, such as the heart or liver.

Further Reading

Allen, Susan J. *Tutankhamen's Tomb: The Thrill of Discovery.* New York, NY: The Metropolitan Museum of Art, 2006.

Alva, Walter and Maria Longhena. *The Incas and Other Andean Civilizations.* San Diego, CA: Thunder Bay Press, 2000.

Barber, Elizabeth Wayland. *The Mummies of Urumchi.* New York, NY: W.W. Norton & Company, 1999.

Brannen, Sarah S., and Christine Liu-Perkins. *At Home in Her Tomb: Lady Dai and the Ancient Chinese Treasures of Mawangdui.* Watertown, MA: Charlesbridge, 2014.

Fowler, Brenda. *Iceman: Uncovering the Life and Times of a Prehistoric Man Found in an Alpine Glacier.* Chicago, IL: University of Chicago Press, 2007.

Hong, Jeehee. *Theater of the Dead: A Social Turn in Chinese Funerary Art, 1000–1400.* Honolulu, III: University of Hawai'i Press, 2016.

Hsing, I-tien, and Zhixin Sun. *Age of Empires: Art of the Qin and Han Dynasties.* New York, NY: Metropolitan Museum of Art, 2017.

Mair, Victor H. *The Tarim Mummies: Ancient China and the Mystery of the Earliest Peoples from the West.* New York, NY: Thames & Hudson, 2000.

Portal, Jane. *The First Emperor: China's Terracotta Army.* Cambridge, MA: Harvard University Press, 2007.

Potthoff, Stephen F. *The Afterlife in Early Christian Carthage: Near-Death Experiences, Ancestor Cult, and the Archaeology of Paradise.* (Routledge Studies in the Early Christian World.) New York, NY: Routledge—Taylor & Francis Group, 2017.

Shoup III, John A. *The Nile: An Encyclopedia of Geography, History, and Culture.* Santa Barbara, CA: ABCE-CLIO, 2017.

Venit, Marjorie Susan. *Visualizing the Afterlife in the Tombs of Graeco-Roman Egypt.* New York, NY: Cambridge University Press, 2016.

Weeks, Kent R., and Richard H. Wilkinson. *The Oxford Handbook of the Valley of the Kings.* New York, NY: Oxford University Press, 2016.

Wilkinson, Richard H. *Pharoah's Land and Beyond: Ancient Egypt and Its Neighbors.* New York, NY: Oxford University Press, 2017.

WEBSITES

The Afterlife in Ancient Egypt

http://www.pbs.org/wgbh/nova/ancient/afterlife-ancient-egypt.html

In this article from PBS, an Egyptologist answers various questions about ancient Egyptian burial practice, covering everything from the practical details of mummification to the metaphysical beliefs that inspired the process.

Europe's Famed Bog Bodies Are Starting to Reveal Their Secrets

http://www.smithsonianmag.com/science-nature/europe-bog-bodies-reveal-secrets-180962770

This article from Smithsonian Magazine goes into great detail about what researchers currently know about bog bodies—in particular Tolland Man—and the technology that enables them to find out more about their origins. The article includes a map of where bog bodies have been found and images of the research process.

The Griffith Institute

http://www.griffith.ox.ac.uk/gri/4tut.html/

This site contains the complete record of Howard Carter's excavation of Tutankhamon's tomb, including Harry Burton's photographs of the process.

Mummies Around the World—Dried, Smoked, or Thrown in a Bog

http://news.nationalgeographic.com/2016/01/160118-mummies-world-bog-egypt-science

National Geographic gives an overview of the place of mummies in cultures around the world. The article also describes the mummification techniques used by different cultures and provides photographs of notable examples.

Index